Organizational Crisis Management

Organizational Crisis Management

The Human Factor

Gerald Lewis

Auerbach Publications
Taylor & Francis Group
Boca Raton   New York

Auerbach Publications is an imprint of the
Taylor & Francis Group, an informa business

Published in 2006 by
Auerbach Publications
Taylor & Francis Group
6000 Broken Sound Parkway NW, Suite 300
Boca Raton, FL 33487-2742

International Standard Book Number-10: 0-8493-3962-6 (Hardcover)
International Standard Book Number-13: 978-0-8493-3962-2 (Hardcover)
Library of Congress Card Number 2005058145

Library of Congress Cataloging-in-Publication Data

Lewis, Gerald W., 1950-
　　Organizational crisis management : the human factor / Gerald Lewis.
　　　　p. cm.
　　Includes bibliographical references and index.
　　ISBN 0-8493-3962-6 (alk. paper)
　　1. Crisis management. 2. Emergency management. 3. Disasters--Psychological aspects. I. Title.

HD49.L525 2006
658.4'77--dc22　　　　　　　　　　　　　　　　　　　　　　　　　　2005058145

Taylor & Francis Group
is the Academic Division of Informa plc.

Visit the Taylor & Francis Web site at
http://www.taylorandfrancis.com

and the Auerbach Publications Web site at
http://www.auerbach-publications.com

Contents

Appendices

Preface

It has been more than eleven years since writing my first book, *Critical Incident Stress and Trauma in the Workplace,* and about seven since co-authoring *Workplace Violence: Myth and Reality* with Dr. Nancy Zare. Since then, we have seen many dramatic events, some of them earth shattering as well as heart breaking. To note a few: terrorism in the form of the Murrah Building, the Atlanta Olympic bomb, and 9/11; infrastructure problems such as mass power outages and Y2K; natural disasters in the form of hurricanes and earthquakes; and organizational crises such as the Enron debacle, as well as the shift in the economy that has resulted in the "dot.com" boom going to the "dot.gone" exodus. While homicide in the workplace has actually diminished significantly, we continue to bear witness to incidents such as Edgewater Technologies. Schools, often thought of as a safe haven, have continued to experience mass murder in libraries and classrooms.

As a country, we are in the midst of a significant transmutation in the culture: a presidential impeachment; a presidential election whose legality was questioned; a "preemptive" war. New terms such as "detainees," "Gitmo," "weapons of mass destruction," "IEDs," "Homeland Security," and "the 9/11 Commission" have become common in the lexicon. New practices such as taking off shoes at airports and removing computers from cases are experienced as little more than inconveniences. Issues such as gay marriage, illegal immigrants, and abortion continue to remain a staple of intense political and social discussion. The country has polarized politically as well as religiously in a way that has not been experienced in quite some time.

Yet, work organizations carry on in an economy that is also going through a significant modification. During the past ten years we have seen the Dow Jones go as high as 11,000 and then drop after 9/11… to rise again like the phoenix. Gas has reached its highest price in the history

ix

of this country. Work organizations continue to experience a myriad of tumultuous shifts and changes demonstrated by major downsizing, reorganizations, mergers and acquisitions, and closings. Outsourcing to foreign countries has continued to decimate the ranks of many work organizations. Government policies and policing have resulted in a significant amount of work for certain groups.

We are also seeing the maturation of a new field — that of business/organizational continuity and a new professional identity — that goes by many different labels. For the purpose of this book, I call it the "organizational continuity planner." The field, while perhaps not in its infancy, remains in its adolescence as it struggles to make sense of a new world, new crises, and the greater need for compliance. While certain work settings might be more focused on one aspect of information continuity and disaster management, others look at security and workflow continuation. From IT offices to educational institutions, from healthcare settings to financial organizations, from the public to the private sector, all must focus on how to maintain operations in the face of a wide range of disruptions. People have arrived at these positions from a wide scope of professions. Some took the road from information technology (IT), while others came the way of security. Some journeyed through Human Resources while others were drawn from Operations or Finance. Currently, the field is an amalgamation of professions with a tendency to have a myopic focus dependent on their specific training as well as the unique concerns of their work organization. Yet they all have one common goal: how to keep operations moving regardless of whether it is a hospital or a school, a financial or factory setting, or a local or national company.

I also have taken a journey. Since the 1980s and 1990s, I have probably provided more than 500 critical incident or trauma debriefings and other interventions to a wide range of work settings. However, I discovered that this was not enough. Often providing a debriefing was a positive experience for the participants, but the organization needed more. I would find myself sitting with management, discussing strategies for them to continue to help their workforce after a significant event. In addition, the management would express its own issues and reactions; and while we were calling it "consultation," it was often a "debriefing" of that level of personnel. What struck me was that many well-meaning people were quite often stuck not knowing what to do or how to do it. It also became obvious that any intervention that took place in the first week or so after an event did not do much for the reactions that were to emerge three to four months later. In addition, while individuals may need one type of intervention, the total organization as a system requires yet a different level of service. What I also witnessed was the level of confusion and chaos that often ensued as a result of little to no planning. While major efforts may have been made to develop prevention and mitigation strategies for the IT systems, or huge amounts of monies spent on hard security, little had been done to consider the impact on personnel. What became obvious in short order was what I describe as: "an organization can get its phone lines back up and have its computers backed up … but its workers may still be screwed up."

This book is the culmination of what I have learned in working with people in employment settings who have received "on-the-job training" in crisis management. These are people and work organizations that have experienced tragedy, trauma, and the ensuing turmoil. I have peppered this book with references, research, and documentation, but it is intended to be more of a "nuts-and-bolts" effort that the reader can immediately apply to his or her work setting.

In addition, I must take a moment to comment on one of the major pathways that opened up for me on this journey, one that was truly the inspiration for writing this book. A couple of years ago, I was approached by Boston University (BU). At the time, the university was in the planning stages of developing an online graduate program in Emergency Management and Organizational Continuity. I was invited to develop the course that became The Social and Psychological Elements of Workplace Disruption. Since then, I was appointed the Faculty Coordinator for the program, which soon will move from a four-course certificate program to a master's level degree program. Two important comments must be made: (1) BU, a highly respected educational institution saw the "writing on the wall" in terms of the need for this kind of education; and (2) BU was willing to devote an entire course to the "human factor."

I would like to dedicate this to all those people who have shared with me their experiences, taught me significant lessons, and allowed me the opportunity to share this with others. In addition, I would like to include all of those students who have chosen to devote personal and professional resources to pursuing this as an academic career and from whom I continue to learn a great deal.

Gerald Lewis, Ph.D.

Introduction

This book intends to provide both theoretical background as well as practical strategies for responding to workplace crises. While many professionals are quite competent when dealing with operational aspects of organizational continuity, often the "human factor" does not receive adequate attention. This book provides a comprehensive understanding of the ubiquitous yet complex reactions of the workforce to a wide array of organizational disruptions.

The focus of Chapters 1 and 2 is on understanding the rapid historical changes that have recently taken place and the current state of the workplace milieu. These chapters introduce the reader to the necessity of understanding the workplace culture, the industry-specific dynamics of different work settings, the fragility of employee motivation and morale, and the toxicity that occurs in any employment setting as well as the dramatic impact of crises on all of the aforementioned variables.

While most business contingency plans focus on operations, Chapter 3 provides a methodology to assess the potential impact of different categories of crises on the workforce. In addition, this chapter begins to delve into some pre-incident mitigation strategies.

Chapters 4 and 5 explore the psychological reactions of individuals as well as groups who have experienced a wide range of personal and professional crises. The content also describes the stages and phases through which individuals, families, communities, and workgroups traverse, often taking up to two to three years to reach a stable resolution. Once again, efforts are made to impart pre-incident policies and plans as well as post-incident services and interventions.

Chapter 6 investigates the impact of the "Five Rs": **Remaining** at home; **Retaining** at work (sheltering in place); **Releasing** to home or a shelter; **Relocating** to a new facility; **Returning** to a previous workplace. Be it a natural disaster, a power outage, downsizing, or terrorism, an organization may be forced to displace workers, which results in a major disruption. This chapter describes some pre- and post-transition strategies.

Chapter 7 looks at the legal and security aspects of workplace disruption. Events ranging from workplace violence to sexual harassment, from layoffs to litigation, are discussed from a legal and security perspective.

Chapter 8 details specific services, programs, and interventions that should be in place prior to any event. In addition, guidelines are set forth for working with the media, emergency management agencies, and behavioral health services.

The Workbook appendices provide the capstone of the book. Appendix A provides a nuts-and-bolts application to a number of different scenarios. It is designed to replicate a tabletop exercise or simulation, allowing the reader or a team to walk through an evaluation process, assess the human factor impact, and then derive strategies and services to implement. Appendix B asks the reader to do an assessment of his or her own work organization culture as well as the Organizational Continuity Team and plan(s).

About the Author

Gerald Lewis, Ph.D., is an international organizational consultant and trainer who has worked with government agencies, healthcare facilities, educational settings, and private businesses on a wide range of work, behavioral health, and organizational issues.

He has authored numerous articles and two books: *Critical Incident Stress and Trauma in the Workplace* (1994) and *Workplace Hostility: Myth & Reality* (co-author, 1998). In addition, he contributed the chapter entitled "Violence at Work: Causes and Protection" in *Psychopathology in the Workplace: Recognition and Adaptation,* edited by J. Thomas and M. Hersen (2004).

He is an Assistant Adjunct Professor and serves as the Faculty Coordinator of the Emergency Management and Organizational Continuity Program at Boston University and teaches one of its courses, "The Social and Psychological Impact of Workplace Disruption."

He provides litigation consultation and expert testimony involving workplace issues in the areas of post-traumatic stress disorder (PTSD), sexual harassment, workplace violence, fitness for duty, negligent retention/ termination, Americans with Disabilities, malpractice, depression, drug and alcohol issues, etc.

Chapter 1

Understanding the Work Organization as a Social Milieu

Take a look at the changes that have taken place in the American workplace and workforce over the past several decades. As described in *A Nation at Work* by Schaffner and Van Horn: "Compared with three or four decades ago, the U.S. workforce is composed of more women, more minorities, more immigrants, more non-union workers, more service workers, and more educated workers."[1] Specifically:

- The proportion of women at work grew from 32 percent in 1948 to more than 60 percent in 2000.
- In 1960, foreign-born workers comprised about 6 percent of the workforce and now make up about 13 percent, and this percentage continues to increase.
- The hallmark of U.S. productivity, manufacturing of all types of products, has dropped to about 13 percent of all jobs.
- Further, U.S. workers are logging in more hours on the job than any other Western industrialized nation while receiving fewer benefits than their predecessors received.
- In 1950, six out of ten workers were considered unskilled. Now that trend has reversed, with the majority of workers being more highly educated. In fact, it is now estimated that 25 percent of all jobs require at least an associates degree, and this is expected to jump to 40 percent by 2008.

1

- In 1954, 35 percent of workers were employed in union positions whereas in 2000, those numbers had dropped to about 13 percent.
- Finally, the American worker is older. For the first time in documented history, there will be more workers over the age of 40 than under the age of 40 as the baby boomer generation ages.

In 1956, William Whyte of *Fortune* magazine described the "Organization Man."[2] He (there really were no organizational women in 1960) was well known in the American community as the abundance of veterans returning from World War II and Korea blithely traded their military uniforms for work uniforms, be it a tie and jacket or a set of boots and overalls. They would return to their hometown, find employment, a wife, and a home relatively close to where they had grown up. They would go to their place of employment and hopefully rise within its ranks while devoting years of service to the company. There was an unwritten contract that defined the relationship between worker and workplace: you remain loyal to the organization, and the organization will take care of you and your family. Workdays usually were delineated by clear boundaries. People would report to a specific place at a specific time and do a specific job reporting to a specific boss. At the end of the day, they would return to their homes, leaving their work at the office or factory and settle in for a night of personal priority. In general, they would work with the same group of individuals for some time before moving to another location or position. When they reached the designated age of retirement, they would leave with benefits that acknowledged their years of service. The TV sitcoms of the 1950s through 1970s, as characterized by shows such as *My Three Sons, Leave It to Beaver,* and *Father Knows Best,* were populated by these men. While this description may seem a bit too simplistic and perhaps naive, it was the environment in which many of today's current workforce grew up.

This is quite a change from the current baby boomer employee of today who, on average, will work for seven different companies during her 40+ years of employment. She may work from her home or be in a group that is constantly shifting and transforming. The hierarchical loyalty to the organization has been replaced by a sense of mutual commitment to a time-limited contract or task-oriented project. Rather than building cars, workers are providing service and information in cubicles that tend to isolate them from others. The water cooler, cafeteria, or lunchroom has been replaced with eating at one's desk, running personal errands, or perhaps going to the in-house gym. People's bosses may be in an office down the hall or just as likely may be in an office across the country. This author consulted with numerous individuals who have never met their boss directly, but speak by phone or communicate via e-mail instead.

Whereas the organization man *of old* was hired by his boss and, in fact, was often known to his new boss because they had worked in the same organization for numerous years, today's worker may have entered the company via a placement agency, Human Resources department, or head hunter with limited direct input from her immediate supervisor.

Technology: Our Love/Hate Relationship

The rapid influx of technology has blurred what was the concrete boundary of the workplace. Cell phones, pagers, computers, PDAs, Wi-Fi modems, fax machines, Webcams, and conference calls have facilitated the development of virtual offices. People can work from anywhere (including coffee shops, airports, and hotels) at any time with anyone in any place in the world. Most of the message slips from secretaries have been replaced by direct e-mails. Numerous people have told this author that it is easier to check e-mail while on vacation than be overwhelmed by the hundreds of messages waiting for them upon their return to work. For many in service and sales, the need to be in constant touch with the office has become the rule, not the exception, thus creating a blurred boundary that keeps the individual "on call" most of the time. Restaurants, movie theaters, museums, and other public places have established policies requesting that individuals refrain from using their phones and pagers. Most every conference or workshop now is initiated by a request that people put their phones on vibrate so as not to disrupt the program. Complaints from family members that "she is always on the phone" or "he is always working" have become a very common component of the modern American family. It must be noted that technology is certainly not all bad and has, in fact, provided a greater degree of freedom by allowing people to telecommute or do their business directly and with greater speed. I can remember when I was the Chief Psychologist at a hospital and carried a pager (the old fashion kind). If I were driving in my car and the pager went off, I would have to pull off the road to find a pay phone, call the service to receive the message, then find enough change to call the individual who had paged me, and I would conduct my business from a public payphone. Now my phone is my paging system, and I can receive a text message from the service, return the call, and never let go of the steering wheel.

While technology has increased the ability to communicate, one might question whether it has increased or diminished the capacity to connect with co-workers in the workplace. It is through feeling this connection that we derive our sense of team, community, attachment, and belonging — all essential aspects of what humans need to feel: valued, respected, and acknowledged. It is these core social and emotional elements that lubricate human beings and keep them going in times of difficulty, be it a personal, professional, or even a national crisis.

From Worker to Employee

While in many respects the conditions of employees have changed dramatically in recent years, these changes have generated a complex and dynamic relationship between employer and employee.

The aforementioned "organizational man" has only been a very recent development in human history. For thousands of years, workers were considered little more than a discardable commodity. From slavery to sweatshops, farms to factories, indentured servitude to in-house servants, the worker was never a highly valued component in the workplace. Working long hours in often-unbearable conditions, being paid a mere pittance, the workers struggled with none of the benefits that are now considered commonplace. They would struggle to maintain their job despite these adversities because they understood the contract: "If you don't or can't work, we will find someone else to fill your position. Do not complain even in the face of discrimination, sexual harassment, violence, and intolerable working conditions." And for hundreds of generations throughout the world, this was standard. For a relatively short duration in human experience, there was a dramatic shift that began around the turn of the 20th century. Labor unions, civil rights legislation, employment policies, psychology, two world wars, and governmental intervention came together in a dramatic confluence that resulted in a shift that the workplace had not seen in modern work history. Workers became employees, personnel, staff, teams, signaling the acknowledgment that the people in the workplace were not a disposable commodity, but rather an essential element of the workplace. The new paradigm was that employees should be developed, nurtured, and cultivated. Employees should receive salaries and benefits. Vacation, sick leave, disability, bonuses, pension plans, and health insurance became common staples in the American workplace. Jobs should become careers or professions. A personal covenant between worker and workplace developed. Most of us grew up in this work environment, and we do not realize that this change was hard fought (often including violence) yet extremely rapid when viewed from a long-term perspective.

The History of Management

Along with this recent change came the study of *organizational behavior,* defined as "the study of human behavior, attitudes, and performance within an organizational setting; drawing on theory, methods, and principles from such disciplines as psychology, sociology, and cultural anthropology to learn about individual, group, structure, and processes."[3]

While owners and masters, chiefs and leaders, bosses and foremen have been around for millennia, the concepts of organizations, systems, administrators, managers, and supervisors are relatively new. The notion that human behavior at work should be studied, and that management should have principles and theories, developed a little more than 100 years ago. (It is probably no coincidence that this concurred with the beginning works of Freud, Jung, and other pioneers in the study of human psychology.) During the mid-1800s when this country was fully ensconced in the industrial revolution, the need to look at improving how people worked was becoming more critical. In 1881, Joseph Wharton gifted $100,000 to the University of Pennsylvania to study management. In 1886, Frederick Taylor presented a paper entitled "The Engineer as an Economist," in which he expressed his thoughts on "scientific management."[4] Regarded by many as the father of present-day management, he developed four critical principles, roughly summarized as:

1. Develop a science for each element of an employee's work.
2. Train, teach, and develop the worker.
3. Management and the worker should cooperate.
4. Develop a sense of equality between management and labor in division of responsibility for the work.

More than 100 years later, these remain viable concepts for modern-day managers.

In the early 1900s, Henri Fayol, a French industrialist, presented the idea that management could be learned and taught and that colleges should begin to offer courses in such knowledge.[5]

These individuals, among others, began the shift in understanding and knowledge that developing skills in managing the workforce could prove a viable strength and might lead to a greater level of productivity. Now this might seem pretty straightforward, but at the time it was a provocative concept. Further, this notion would lead to the development of concepts such as organizational behavior, organizational development, work culture, cross training, and the works of individuals such as Deming, Covey, Blanchard, etc. More recently, in *Workplace Psychopathology* (2004), Jon Frew writes of the work done by Hunsaker and Alessandra in 1986: "The art of managing others is a dynamic process that is ever changing and evolving. Many of the managerial concepts proposed only a few years ago cannot and will not work in today's environment. People have changed. Government has changed. The world has changed." Frew continues on to say: "Into the 1980s and 1990s, the fundamental fabric of the management role has been torn away. Managers who were once expected to command, control, and persuade others to engage in activities they would not do if not closely watched were now required to be leaders, to be forward thinking, to have people skills, and to build self-managed teams."[6] What factors came to coordinate for this rapid change in the workplace would take too much time to discuss in this book. However, to label a few, technology, the change from manufacturing to service and information, the baby boomer generation with its sense of empowerment (or perhaps, entitlement) that grew from the 1960s, civil rights, and diversity in the workplace are some of the major influences.

The old adage in politics states that "all politics is local." Well, in a similar way, *all productivity is the individual.* With an increasingly diverse workforce, understanding the individual characteristics of workers, how to motivate them, how to maintain a level of satisfaction, and how to mitigate the build-up of stress and strain in the individual and within the group has become an essential task. As many supervisors acknowledge, 90 percent of the time is spent managing 10 percent of the workforce. In times of crisis and tragedy, the ability to manage a traumatized or anxious workgroup may be overwhelming for any level of management.

Organizational Culture

To understand a workgroup or any group of people, it is necessary to understand the culture. Most of us live in numerous cultures at one time. We may be brought up in a family culture, that is part of a community culture, which is part of a regional culture, and is within a national culture. We have gender cultures and we might belong to a religious group and go to work in an office, factory, retail, healthcare, or governmental setting — each with its own type of culture. We might have children who bring yet another culture to us. We might belong to sports teams or activity groups, each with its own culture. Most are able to find a way to manage the multitude of cultures in which they find themselves. They can modify their identity and behaviors as they transition from one culture to the other. It is when cultures clash that the individual feels caught in a bind. Let us look at cultures because nothing can potentially generate change to a culture more than a crisis.

The word "culture" derives from the term "cultivate": to grow, nurture, care for. The development of a culture is an amazingly complex and ever-changing process. Whenever groups of people come together, basic values, attitudes, behaviors, and expectations develop that tend to exert an influence on the individuals who compose the group. Be it a tribal village in Africa, a cellblock in a prison, a fraternity on a college campus, or a department within a work organization, the inborn tendency is to develop a culture. Cultural differences can be described using four terms: *symbols, heroes, rituals,* and *values.* Symbols are language, gestures, or artifacts that are unique to the culture and are imbued with special meaning. Examples are eagles and flags, crucifixes, and stars. Heroes "are persons alive or dead, real or imaginary, who possess characteristics which are highly prized in the culture and become a model for behavior."[7] Examples are Jesus and Moses, George Washington and Martin Luther King. Rituals are "collective activities that are technically superfluous, but which within the culture are considered socially essential."[8] Examples are holidays, handshakes, religious ceremonies, parades, etc. There is usually a document or body of verbal stories that delineate the cultural norms. Examples are the Bible, Koran, Constitution, and the Bill of Rights — or pledges, corporate mission statements, etc., or myths, stories, or legends. These documents or stories have been passed down through the ages, having been studied, interpreted, and revered from generation to generation. They are usually looked toward at times of turmoil and unrest as a way of assuaging apprehension and anxiety among the group.

The bottom line of any culture is that it establishes norms and thus a sense of identity and stability. The balance between fluidity and rigidity in a culture is a constant dynamic. Systems that tend to be more fluid may be better able to respond to external changes, new information, and tend to incorporate components of other cultures as they evolve. The "downside" to a culture characterized as fluid is that there may be a tendency toward an individualistic orientation that might result in difficulty for the group to respond cohesively to an overwhelming crisis. A system that is considered more rigid has a difficult time incorporating new realities or evidence that calls into question some of the basic tenets of the culture. Within these cultures, there is a tendency to adhere to the norms, even in the face of evidence that may be contradictory. For example, several hundred years ago, it was the cultural norm to believe that the earth was the center of the universe and to say otherwise was heresy, punishable by death. Galileo, the father of astronomy, was punished severely for preaching that the sun rather than the earth was the center of the solar system, a concept that we now take for granted. It took years of repeated scientific evidence to shift the paradigm to that of a *solar-centric* system. In a similar manner, for hundreds of years, this country's culture held that African Americans were less than equal and it was (and still is, in some places) the norm to discriminate against them. Speaking in generalities, a scientific or academic culture may tend to be more fluid, seeking out new data and incorporating new findings into its theories and beliefs. Religious and military cultures tend to be more closed and rigid, often struggling with and fighting against new information, be it technological or trendy. Fluid systems tend to be more oriented toward the individual while rigid systems promote the group. Rigid systems tend to foster a sense of belonging to a larger group identity, which may be comforting at times of severe crisis, yet also fostering a sense of dependency and an expectation of adherence to the rules of the culture. Fluid systems work better at times of *smooth sailing*, allowing for a greater tolerance of individual differences and creativity. A culture creates a sense of stability and identity for members within the group and facilitates strategies to manage the turmoil and travails of a group.

Taking this a bit deeper, norms and values are established by a culture and are its basic building blocks. Values can be defined as "the conscious affective desires or wants of people that guide behavior.... Values are a group's ideas about what is right or wrong.... Values are passed down from one generation to the next and are communicated through education systems, religion, families, communication and organizations." Be it a country, a workplace, or an army, "cultures sustain people throughout periods of difficulty and serve to ward off anxiety."[9] Further, with respect to the workplace, "organizations are able to operate efficiently only when shared values exist among the employees."[10]

As indicated previously, cultures are always responding to internal and external events and therefore are in a constant state of evolution. Be it a family or a nation, a workplace or religious group, crises and tragedies often provide a compelling stimulus for changes in a culture and its norms and values. The question then arises: does organizational culture evolve on its own on an unconscious level, or can it be influenced or actively changed? As reported by Ivancevich and Matteson, typically there are five steps to influencing a cultural shift: (1) get people to change their behavior; (2) by helping them to understand the value of the change in behavior; (3) through communication about changes via a number of modalities, including rewarding those who comply with the changes; (4) as new people enter the system, they do so with the new behaviors in place; (5) while removing old members who are unwilling or unable to comply with the new behavioral expectations.[11] Fortunately or unfortunately, we witness this all the time in government and in the workplace. While this book is being edited, we are seeing it in our own country as the cabinet members of one administration are resigning and being replaced by new people who are culturally more akin to the president's desired cultural norms.

Nothing can impact a culture quite like a crisis. It is essential to understand the pre-crisis culture of any type of organization. By doing so, one may be able to formulate some pre-incident strategies to mitigate the impact. However, often an organization continues blithely along until it comes to an incident and then (over)reacts to the situation out of haste and anxiety.

Lord of the Flies: A Case Example of a Traumatized Culture

A well-known and notable work of literature that describes the evolution of a culture among young boys marooned on an island was the book (and later a movie), *Lord of the Flies*.[12] While the book covered many provocative aspects of human behavior, one perspective was about the desire for, the war between, and the pressure to live within a culture that had been impacted by tragedy. Cultures are defined as "[a] pattern of basic assumptions — invented, discovered, or developed by a given group as it learns to cope with problems of external adaptation and internal integration."[13] If tolerated, the internal integration process within a culture may allow for the establishment of different groups within the organization, as seen in religious practices, different political parties, etc. Or, in a more rigid system, the organization may be void of obvious variations, as in totalitarian regimes and fundamental religious groups. At times, the internal integration process may reach dramatic proportions, resulting in open struggle such as civil war, governmental coups, or "hostile takeovers" as one internal culture attempts to dominate another.

I would recommend to the reader renting the recent movie version of *Lord of the Flies* and watching the group as they struggle to maintain the old values of their culture, while they face fear of terrorism (the "monster in the cave"), abandonment by their government, splitting between factions, and new norms, values, rituals, heroes, and myths. What is Jack's role? Piggy's? Ralph's? What do the youngins' represent? What about the conch? The fire? The monster? Living in America since 9/11, does this have any familiarity to it? As this book is being written, one of the top TV shows in America is the series *Lost*; a modern-day *Lord of the Flies*. Once again, a group of people is marooned on an island after a plane crash with all of the attendant dynamics and personal issues, including an unseen monster in the bush, the hope for rescue, and the development of factions. Taking this concept a bit further, the success of the TV series *Survivor* is yet another example of crises, challenges, and the impact on the evolving culture of the tribes and the members. One could spend much time looking at the tribe-versus-tribe dynamic, the names and colors of each tribe, the loss of members, the infighting between members, the merging of tribes, the rituals such as the tribal counsel, etc., and the loss of members as they are voted out. It is no wonder that since 9/11 these types of "reality" shows have generated such a resonance with the viewing public. Once again, they are examples of how humans cope with crisis, character, and relational dynamics.

A business continuity planner must think about how a potential crisis could impact the workplace culture. How will it affect the values and attitudes? Does the workplace have a fluid or rigid culture? How has it dealt with crises in the past? The past may often be a prelude to the future. If not a prelude, then certainly a valuable opportunity to learn.

Motivation and Morale

During times of crisis, maintaining motivation and morale of the workforce is a vital aspect to business continuity. As stated previously, the focus of management has changed significantly in recent years. Most management articles and books indicate that the critical priority in today's fast-paced occupational environment is to have managers work to improve the motivation of their employees under the assumption that motivated employees make better and more productive employees. So the question remains: how can a work organization improve employee motivation? In the face of increased work demand, layoffs, reorganizations, consistent transitions, and turmoil — what this author refers to as "terror-phobia" (tongue-in-cheek for the current level of apprehension that is being experienced around the potential for terrorism) — how can motivation and morale be maintained, let alone increased?

Since the times of Wharton, Fayol, and Taylor, there has been a shift in the workplace culture. We see mission statements and learned experts promoting concepts such as "empowerment," "communication," "develop your workers," "commit to people-first values," and "teamwork," yet very few organizations actually *walk the talk*. It is this author's opinion that it is better for an organization to say nothing than to "promote" these types of values or concepts and to then not to facilitate them among the workforce or put them into practice. In recent history, most countries and workplaces adhere to an understanding that, within a certain framework, their leaders will conduct themselves by the same rules and regulations as are expected of them. While there is a certain degree of flexibility and an understanding that the higher up the "feeding chain" of an organization one's rank, there are certain "privileges." However, it is a subtle yet very powerful experience of betrayal when people in a position of power indicate that they are conducting themselves and their organizations under certain statutes, expectations, or protocols and the experienced reality of the community (be it a church group, workgroup, or political group) is something far different. Examples abound of this type of malversation, be it a president lying about a sexual relationship with an intern, a priest preaching religion while abusing the children of parishioners, a CEO living the high life while the company and its pension plans go down the tubes, a Viet Nam veteran who puts himself in harm's way only to return to a country that treats him like an enemy, or any number of smaller examples that occur so often in so many ways. Feeling betrayed leads to a loss of trust. A loss of trust may lead to a sense of isolation and existential loneliness or a fomenting sense of rage that may be self-or other-directed. In times of crisis and tragedy, any culture and the individuals within it are vulnerable to these experiences. Thus, to counter this natural tendency, strategies to nurture trust and a sense of community must be a key component of any response plan.

If this is the case, how does one maintain or improve the motivation and morale of the workforce when it is faced with a crisis? For the moment, these terms are being used interchangeably; however, later we look at the relationship between motivation and morale as they actually connote two different but related concepts.

As mentioned previously, the study of human behavior developed into an organized "soft science" a little more than 100 years ago. In the early years, the *new* field of psychology spent much time attempting to determine the building blocks of human behavior. The Freudian school thought that much was the result of upbringing and early childhood experience that greatly influenced one's intelligence, motivation, behavior, and subsequent emotional disorders. Later, the Behaviorists thought that it was all about learning and conditioning. Drawing on experiments conducted with a wide variety of subjects ranging from rats to humans, their theories held that if you reward certain behaviors, you could *condition* the animal or human to repeat them. If you punished or did not reward behaviors, the behaviors would be diminished or in their language "extinguished." For years the battle waged between the psychodynamic model versus the behavioral model. Now it is understood that behavior is much more complex than can be measured along this dichotomous dynamic. There are many factors that influence behavior. Certainly, upbringing and early experience, as well as conditioning, are included. In recent years, culture and environmental factors have been viewed as significant determinants. So too have biological and neurological factors.

All orientations believe that one core determinant of human behavior is motivation. What "makes" people do what they do? Why do some become violent, while others demonstrate heroism? Why are some honest, while others are criminal? How come some are good employees while others remain obstructionistic? Certainly, this discussion has waged for decades and is an ongoing area of interest and research in the fields of psychology and sociology and will not be covered sufficiently in this book. However, one of the first researchers to look at motivation in the early part of the 20th century was Abraham Maslow.[14] He determined a theoretical construct suggesting that people were motivated by the goal of satisfying five levels of ascending needs as described in Table 1.1. Further, that once a specific need was satisfied, it no longer served as a

TABLE 1.1   Maslow's Hierarchy of Needs

Self-actualization: the opportunity to utilize one's abilities to their maximum free of constraint
Self-esteem: feeling valued, acknowledged, and appreciated by others
Belongingness, social and love: being with family or a community and feeling a sense of belonging
Safety and security: a safe haven with limited threat of harm
Physiological: food, shelter, clothing, relief from pain

source of motivation. Also, the lack of satisfaction of a need could result in frustration and stress, thus causing inappropriate behavior in an effort to satisfy those needs.

Being realistic, it is not expected that any individual truly reaches the ultimate satisfaction of all of his or her needs. Typically, most people get 85 percent of physiological, 70 percent of safety and security, 50 percent of belonging, 40 percent of esteem, and 10 percent of self-actualization needs.[15]

It should be noted that with most activities, more than one level of need is receiving some degree of satisfaction. So, there may be a primary level as well as secondary levels. As an example, working for a living hopefully provides physiological, safety, self-esteem and self-actualization. Depending on the culture, job duties, and salary, different levels of need may be satisfied in greater proportion.

Table 1.2 looks at a range of behaviors and categorizes at least two levels of satisfaction. One should note that of all of the above activities, work is one that tends to impact on all levels of need satisfaction. (1 represents primary need and 2 indicates secondary levels of need satisfaction.)

Maslow at Work

Applying this to the work milieu, one can once again look to the organizational culture to determine if it promotes the satisfaction of these needs or if it thwarts and frustrates them. Table 1.3 describes Maslow's hierarchy related to the job.[16] This author has taken the liberty of adding those italicized activities.

Think about how one's workplace satisfies or does not satisfy the ascending needs of the workforce. Because most jobs currently take care of the first two levels of needs (physiological and safety/security), people find that they work to satisfy and thus experience the most frustration

TABLE 1.2 Activities Satisfying Level(s) of Need

Activity	1 Physiological	2 Safety and Security	3 Belonging, Social and Love	4 Self-esteem	5 Self-actualization
Eating	1	2	2		
Mating	1		2	2	2
Praying		1	2	2	2
Seeking shelter from a storm	1	2			
Working	1	2	2	2	2
Sleeping	1				
Fighting	1			2	
Rock concert			1		2
Cuddling			1	2	2
Giving birth	1		2	2	2
Exercising				1	2
Child playing with friend			1	2	
Teenager putting on makeup			1	2	2
Person getting a tattoo			1	2	2
Listening to music				1	2
Yoga	2		1	2	2

attempting to ease the upper-level needs. However, during a workplace crisis or tragedy, there may be a significant downward shift in the level of needs. With the worry about terrorism, for a while people were less concerned with self-esteem and actualization and more focused on safety and security. At times of a layoff, one may experience the same shift from "My job doesn't empower and challenge me" to "I hope I have my job next week."

As an example, take a manufacturing company that is very structured and hierarchical in its orientation. There is not a lot of flexibility, and people feel like they are "cogs in a machine." The company employs

TABLE 1.3 Maslow's Hierarchy of Need Satisfaction and the Workplace

Self-actualization:
Challenging assignments
Development opportunities
Opportunities to use skill set

Esteem:
Job title and position
Promotions
Acknowledgment by others
Office furnishings and location
Merit salary increases
Lack of role conflict

Belongingness:
Compatible workgroups
Employee-centered supervision
Labor unions
Personal and professional friends
Office parties and social gatherings

Safety and Security:
General salary increases
Pension plans
Benefits
Insurance
Comfortable physical surroundings
Security and safety

Physiological:
Salary
Heating and air conditioning
Safety equipment

about 450 workers. Management keeps to itself and does not communicate very well with non-management workers. The workforce is undereducated and many feel that they stay at their job because they are "trapped by their paycheck." The work is boring and remains very much the same from day to day. Supervisors receive little training, yet there is increasing demand to deliver more product with the same level of workers. In fact, positions have been cut through attrition. Some workers are subject to mandatory overtime of about four hours per week. In addition, some activities have been cut, such as company holiday parties, softball team, etc. Also, benefits have lessened, such as increased employee premiums for health insurance, sick benefits, and being able to carry over vacation days. It is a predominantly all male, mostly white workforce who has been with the company for an average of ten years. Five years ago, there was an effort to unionize the shop, but it was thwarted by management and the ringleaders were eventually let go. Currently, there are rumors that the company may be sold and relocated to another state, but nothing has been determined as yet.

What are the values and norms of this culture? What would you imagine the areas of need fulfillment and dissatisfaction are for this workplace?

Let us develop the relationship between motivation and morale. While much can and has been explored regarding these two concepts, however, we discuss them as related to this material. Put simplistically, **motivation** can be thought of as an internal, individualistic drive or striving to achieve satisfaction. **Morale** is about belonging to a group, one's feeling about the group itself, and one's feelings about oneself as a member of the group. In general, we talk about individuals being motivated and the group or team having good morale. Ideally, one would want individual people to have strong motivation as well as there be good group morale. However, there may be times when these two run counter to each other. Examples from sporting teams are fraught with this type of conflict. Recently, the Los Angeles Lakers had two members who are highly motivated to achieve recognition and notoriety. They are both superstars in their own right, yet they do not get along with each other. (Since this initial writing, one has contracted with another team.) The team is lacking in morale and this has borne out (although they did make it to the playoffs). On the other hand, the New England Patriots have no superstars and yet they are a team that is thought of as having a high level of morale. In fact, at the beginning of each game, they do not enter the playing field with individual announcements, but rather come out as a group. Military boot camps are known to try to diminish the sense of individual motivation to achieve (except to become a part of the team) and to increase the sense of group cohesiveness and group morale; to think of one's self as a member of the team, to care about your comrade, to become a "band of brothers." In systems that have a high level of morale, there may also be a strong degree of individual motivation. Yet, the motivation is to "win one for the Gipper" rather than to take the trophy for one's self.

So, what do motivation and morale have to do with crisis, trauma, and disasters? How does morale connect with the ability to mitigate the emotional impact of serious incidents, be they personal or professional?

People can tolerate quite a bit of trauma, abuse, and neglect as long as they have a sense of community and trust… a sense of belonging and being nurtured by the group, be it a family, a religious organization, a gang, a country, or a workplace. Human beings have quite a reserve of resiliency from which to draw strength as long as the culture has values and rituals to help restore the individuals' sense of well-being and identity. Nothing taps it faster and more dramatically than feeling betrayed by or disconnected from one's family, group, country, or culture. Most people can handle rejection, loss, and disruption as long as they feel that they have a sense of comfort and connection and are being dealt with in a sincere and honest manner.

Put quite simply, when there is a high level of morale within a group, it facilitates the emotional recovery of the group and the individuals within.

Passive and Active Trauma

In his book entitled *I Don't Want to Talk about It,* Terrance Real described that there are two types of trauma: *active* and *passive*.[17] Active trauma is "a boundary violation, a clearly toxic interaction" — or, put another way the actual injury, assault, surgery, loss of a job, crisis, etc. Passive trauma is "a form of physical or emotional neglect"[18] — the lack of response, nurturance, support that the individual may need but not receive in order to cope with the active trauma. During my workshops I use an example that is probably familiar to many: Imagine a two- to three-year-old child running around a playground. Suddenly, he trips and falls and scrapes his knee and elbow. He picks himself up, and what is the first thing that is done before he actually starts to cry? Most attendees of the workshop respond: "Looks for his mother." I usually chide them that fathers are quite capable as well, but that they are correct… the child looks for a source of nurturance… and then begins to cry. If the source of nurturance were to reject or admonish the child with statements such as: "I told you not to run around or you'd get hurt," or, "Be a big boy, don't cry," or, "I'm too busy right now." These responses would be examples of passive trauma. One may extrapolate from this minor example to larger ones such as the woman who has surgery for cancer that leaves her disfigured (active trauma) and is responded to by her husband with rejection (passive trauma). Or the worker who is laid off (active trauma) and is treated like a criminal when told to pack his belongings and leave the premises immediately (passive trauma). Or the Viet Nam veteran who spends a year in combat (active), only to return home to a community that does not want to hear of his experience and where he is treated as a war criminal (passive trauma). What is understood quite clearly is that most individuals have the capacity to manage active traumas of significant severity as long as they receive acknowledgment, support, and nurturance.

Taking this concept into the workplace, one can begin to understand that there is a wide array of *active* traumas that take place in the workplace. While the workplace may not be responsible for the active trauma as in the case of a flood, fire, power outage, violent episode, or even a layoff, the difficulty is that the way that the workplace manages the incident may result in a significant degree of passive trauma. Often, the workers receive little to no support or acknowledgment of an event that has impacted them dramatically. Or, a business continuity (BC) plan may be rather thorough and sophisticated with respect to the business operations, but does not look sufficiently at the impact on personnel. Several years ago, I was attending a business continuity conference in which people were discussing a variety of plans that would be implemented in the case of a severe flood. One presenter indicated that his company had spent much time and resources setting up a "remote site" about 150 miles away in which the communications work could be conducted. He then went into elaborate detail about how plans were also made for critical employees to stay in a hotel located close to the remote site. He continued on to describe a very comprehensive plan to maintain business continuity. After his presentation, I approached him and asked if any thought had been given to the families of the "critical employees" and how they (the critical employees) might react to leaving their families and homes to stay in a hotel 150 miles away for an unlimited amount of time. The gentleman smiled and said: "Well, it looked great on paper." This anecdote is mentioned because often a BC or DR (disaster response) plan only goes so far in considering the impact on personnel.

Workplace Toxicity

In 1998, this author co-wrote *Workplace Hostility: Myth and Reality*.[19] It described two concepts that might result in hostility and possibly violence in the workplace. The "at-risk" workplace is that which is vulnerable from hostility and violence from outside. Table 1.4 presents the characteristics of an "at-risk" work establishment.

Examples are convenient stores, liquor stores, taxis, etc. The primary type of violence that is perpetrated upon these types of establishments is robbery. However, often these intended robberies result in an assault on

TABLE 1.4 Characteristics of an "At-Risk" Workplace

Public service
Available cash
Few employees/customers
Isolated/high crime area
Easy access
Open at night
Limited security

TABLE 1.5   Characteristics of a "Toxic" Workplace

Authoritarian management style
Favoritism
Perceived humiliation
Arbitrary/inconsistent decisions
Poor communication
Increased work demands
"Poor" working conditions
Minimal management training
Betrayal and abandonment
Employees feeling trapped in their jobs

or death of an employee. The primary mode of protection from these types of violent episodes is to "harden up" the security within and outside the establishment. Although the number of homicides in the workplace has dropped significantly in the past ten years (from around 1000 to below 800), most of them are the result of robberies of this type.[20] Increasing the number of employees, better lighting, security cameras, etc. are methods used to assure a lesser likelihood of being the victim of this type of violence.

The "toxic" workplace is that which is fraught with tension and turmoil generated from within a work organization. It should be noted that all workplaces suffer from some degree of toxicity. Metaphorically, it is the equivalent of cholesterol or blood pressure in the human body. Both of these conditions are normal and occur naturally. However, if one's blood pressure or cholesterol rises above a certain level, it may portend a vulnerability for some type of serious medical problem. In much the same way, if the toxicity in a workplace rises above a certain level, it too may signal the vulnerability for a wide range of behaviors that could certainly result in a disruption of work continuity. Table 1.5 shows the characteristics of a toxic work organization.

As previously indicated, a certain degree of toxicity is to be expected and can be tolerated by most work organizations. [Using our examples of the sports teams, the Los Angeles Lakers probably have a system that has a higher level of toxicity than that of the New England Patriots]. Toxic systems usually have a lower level of morale, and systems with low morale seem to diminish the motivational levels of individuals… unless it is to leave the group. With a decrease in motivation, one often experiences a decrease in individual performance. As more members of the system experience this cycle, it usually results in a decrease in productivity, more conflicts, diminished communication… and an increase in toxicity. Figure 1.1 describes the circular relationship.

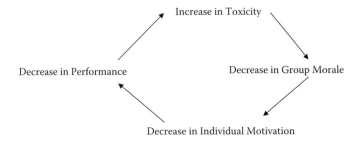

FIGURE 1.1 The toxicity cycle: morale, motivation, performance.

TABLE 1.6 "Normal" Experiences That Increase Organizational Toxicity

Layoff, downsizing, or growth of an organization
Significant increase in work demands
Relocation
Demographic changes
Merger, reorganization
Strikes or protracted labor disputes
High negative visibility media coverage
Individual termination with discipline
Restraining order of a "significant other" of an employee

Toxicity exists in every system. Yet, there are events that can dramatically increase the level and thus the potential for serious harm from within the organization. These events are represented in Table 1.6.

Toxicity can damage morale and a sense of the social work environment. Truax and McDonald (2002) found that poor work relationships, particularly with co-workers, were a risk factor for depression.[21] Conversely, mentoring relationships were found to foster a better social work environment.

Now it must be understood that since 9/11 there is currently great focus on terrorism perpetrated by outsiders (at risk). Prior to that, there seemed to be a number of workplace and school shootings in which an employee or student came to the workplace and randomly shot co-workers (toxic). While statistically the numbers did not amount to a significant percentage of deaths in the workplace, there was a great deal of attention paid to these types of events. It should be noted that there is a wide variety of other types of incidents that occur in the workplace that may not be as notable, given that they do not result in a homicide; however, they take place in much greater numbers and can affect work productivity and in some cases lead to business disruption. See Table 1.7 for a list of those types of events.

TABLE 1.7 Examples of Other Types of Workplace Hostility

Work slowdown (work to rule)
Increased sick leave
Lack of co-worker cooperation and communication
Strikes
Sexual harassment
Intimidation
Violence
Grievances or unnecessary litigation claims
Sabotage
Theft
Destruction of property
Computer hacking, etc.

While weapons of mass destruction and terrorism are of great concern, there is the hope of thwarting these events. However, if one were to look at the aforementioned list, one can expect that several of these have occurred and will continue to occur in any workplace. These also represent hostility in the workplace and a significant potential for operational disruption.

Premorbid Conditions

There is a term in clinical professions called *premorbid condition* or *premorbid history*. It refers to the condition of the organism before it is affected by an accident, disease, or trauma. An individual may be admitted to a hospital to have surgery or as a result of a heart attack. What must be assessed is his or her premorbid condition prior to any intervention. If the individual is healthy, then that must be determined; however, if he has diabetes, is overweight, and has high blood pressure and smokes, these are considered premorbid conditions that must be accounted for and managed prior to any medical intervention or else it may result in a more serious problem. In addition, these premorbid conditions may greatly influence the recovery.

In much the same way, a child may be brought to a mental health professional because she is depressed. An assessment of her premorbid conditions must be ascertained. Perhaps she has a parent who has recently left the home, or a parent who is an alcoholic, or she may have been born prematurely and suffered from anoxia, or her family has recently emigrated from another country, or she sustained a head trauma two weeks ago. These can all be considered premorbid conditions.

Similarly, a workplace is a "living" system with a premorbid history or condition as well. Unfortunately, events that cause workplace disruption do not happen in a vacuum. As discussed, the workplace is a dynamic and evolving culture that is constantly subjected to stressors and changes. These stressors and changes can impact the toxicity and thus the premorbid history. As an example, several years ago I was asked to do a stress management presentation for an organization. I went to the company and quickly discovered that the company was not doing very well financially. Further, there had been a significant demographic change, with the third shift workers now being predominantly an ethnic minority group supervised by a Caucasian supervisor who did not speak their language. Some workers had been laid off and mandatory overtime had been implemented. A year prior, an employee had been seriously injured on the job and had not been able to return to work. These were all events that had increased the toxicity in the organization and thus any presentation on stress management would be "too little, too late." However, the show must go on and I did my PowerPoint slide presentation while the workers sat there with glum, taciturn countenance. Their body language signaled to me: "You've got to be kidding. We've got more than stress." I stopped in the middle of the presentation and opened it up for discussion. Initially, there was limited talk; but within a short amount of time, the floodgates opened and people spoke of their frustrations. Reporting back to upper management that a stress management seminar was not enough to fix the problem was not received with a great deal of excitement. It was akin to telling the overweight, high-blood pressured, smoking, diabetic patient that the surgery could not be performed and would not be successful until and unless he or she got his or her weight and blood pressure down, and sugar under control. I offered further consultation and organizational management training. They thanked me for my input and indicated that they would take it under consideration. Needless to say, I did not hear back from them. Several years later, the company went out of business.

References

1. H. Schaffner and C. Van Horn, *A Nation at Work,* Rutgers University Press, New Brunswick, NJ, 2003, p. 3.
2. *Fortune,* March 16, 1988. Copyright 1998 Time Inc.
3. J. Ivancevich and M. Matteson, *Organizational Behavior and Management,* McGraw-Hill, New York, 2002, p. 10.
4. J. Ivancevich and M. Matteson, *Organizational Behavior and Management,* McGraw-Hill, New York, 2002, p. 9.
5. J. Ivancevich and M. Matteson, *Organizational Behavior and Management,* McGraw-Hill, New York, 2002, p. 9.

Chapter 2

The Relationship between Organizational Culture and Organizational Crisis Management (OCM)

So one might wonder what the relationship is between **organizational culture**, **toxicity**, and **crisis management**. If it is through cultures that values are determined and expressed, if it is through cultures that external events are understood, if it is through cultures that an individual experiences a sense of community and connection, if it is through cultures that one derives a sense of stability and structure, then it is obvious that a crisis management plan must start with an assessment of an organization's culture. As discussed, cultures can be open or closed; they have a premorbid history and a certain level of toxicity. The cycle as described in Figure 1.1 functions to create a downward spiral of toxicity, morale, motivation, and performance. In much the same way that the patient with the bad premorbid history has a medical crisis and requires surgery, a work organization may function very much the same. In the case of our patient, the premorbid history includes bad eating habits, limited exercise, and smoking. The toxicity level is high and, as a result, the patient has developed high blood pressure and high cholesterol, along with a borderline diabetic condition. The different organs within the system (heart, lungs, etc.) are not functioning well, and the morale and motivation of the entire system are diminished ("I know that I should quite smoking and lose weight…"). Even if the surgery were to be "simple," the patient is vulnerable to numerous complications that may be very dangerous to the survival of the individual or, at a minimum, influence the recovery. Metaphorically, the organization might experience the need for "surgery" in the form of a layoff — or, a "medical crisis" that requires immediate intervention, such as a flood or fire. In this case also, the survivability of the organization as well as its recovery is greatly influenced by its premorbid history and the level of toxicity. It may get even more complicated. Assume that the overweight patient with a bad premorbid history with much toxicity lives alone and does not have much in the way of a social system to offer support and care. Statistically, as well as anecdotally, it is understood that social connection at times of stress and strain impact heavily on one's ability to cope. As a reminder, some may have studied Harry Harlow's early work with surrogate monkeys. In this classic experiment, he took newborn monkeys and divided them into two groups. One group was placed with their natural mothers; the other was with "surrogate" monkeys constructed of wire and terry cloth that were rigged to deliver milk to the infant monkeys, but no sense of nurturance. What was discovered was that although both groups received food, the group that had nurturance from the real monkeys was both physically and emotionally healthier. This difference in health continued even after the young monkeys were reunited with real monkeys. Extrapolating from this study, it was postulated that neglect (especially early neglect) with the lack of nurturance can lead to lifelong personality difficulties. Similar findings have been determined with children separated from their parents due to war or illness. Once again returning to the work organization, if there is limited social connection and support, the individuals within as well as the total group may suffer in a similar way.

Imagine this situation: a significant incident happens in a workplace. It could be an explosion, a flood, a downsizing. One of the work sites is a factory, which is a predominantly working-class, male group with the average educational level being high school. The workers have skills that are not useful beyond the type of work they do in the factory. They all have worked together for quite some time, and many live and went to school in the community. A strong social fabric runs among the workers and their families. The factory is a "mom-and-pop" operation that has been owned and run by the same family for three generations. In its heyday, it employed upward of 400 employees and now it has settled at around 250. The management style is friendly and social, yet hierarchical, and people work cooperatively to meet established work orders and deadlines. It is an aging workforce with limited turnover, and many people have worked there for more than 20 years. Workers socialize outside the work setting, and families attend the same schools and religious organizations.

The other work setting is a high-tech computer software firm that has been established for ten years and funded by venture capital. It has a very diverse workforce of 175 people representing a wide range of ethnic groups, ages, and religious affiliations. The majority of workers have a college or graduate-level degree and have not been with the company for any longer than two to three years. Most of the people work as programmers and are between 25 to 35 years of age. Most commute significant distances, and many work from their homes at least one or two days per week. They are highly educated and tend to work alone in their cubicles with limited contact among co-workers. The cultural norm is that "people come and go," moving from one high-tech company to the next as individual opportunities arise. Management style is somewhat laissez-faire, assuming that the individuals are independent and self-motivated.

One can begin to understand how the same event might impact different organizations with different cultures in very different ways, and how the need to have a response plan must take into account the values, expectations, and characteristics as delineated by the culture.

The topic of leadership in times of crisis is discussed in greater detail at another point in this book. However, it is essential to begin to lay the foundation of seeing how the culture and values of an organization must be a central focus of any crisis response. In his book *The Hidden Connections,* Fritjof Capra describes the paradox of the modern-day workplace by asking if it is a "machine for making money" or a "living being."[1] Capra drew on the works of modern-day management theorists such as Peter Senge and Arie De Geus. De Geus wrote *Living Company,* in which he looked at 27 companies that had survived for more than a hundred years. His focus was on determining the unique characteristics that promoted this type of resiliency. His work posited two such characteristics: (1) "a strong sense of community and common identity around a common set of values;"[2] and (2) an openness to the outside world, tolerance for the entry of new individuals and new ideas... and an ability to adapt to new circumstances."[3] De Geus went on to write that when dealing with crises, managers must "shift their priorities from managing companies to optimize capital to managing companies to optimize people."[4]

Definitions of Business Disruption Incidents

While business continuity and disaster management had been evolving for the past several decades, this author suggests that it was not until the mid-1990s, with the growth of high technology, the growing concern about the "millennium bug," and "Y2K," that the field truly began to receive major notoriety and awareness. In a similar vein, 9/11 reconfigured the playing field and brought an even greater awareness of the need to develop response plans for a large-scale event.

Currently, the government and media are predicting the likelihood that a large-scale event such as bioterrorism, or a "dirty bomb" might strike this country. Once again, one can see that a culture determines how a system responds to "problems of external adaptation and internal integration." After 9/11, the values and beliefs of this nation began to shift dramatically. Resources were diverted to new endeavors such as increased security and military resources. Wars were justified and waged in Afghanistan and Iraq. Changes in legislation such as the Patriot Act were passed, allowing for greater tolerance for the law enforcement agencies with respect to investigating individual citizens. New terms entered the lexicon, such as "detainees," "terrorist cells," "dirty bombs," "insurgents," etc. Homeland Security, the 9/11 Commission, a Director of Intelligence (heretofore unknown concepts) became regular topics of our experience. The nation began to experience major struggles with respect to the internal integration that accompanies this type of major shift in culture. Liberal versus conservative, secular versus religious right, Democrat versus Republican, east/west coast versus the midlands — all emerged as the country became polarized in an effort to adapt to a cultural change. In addition, similar to the fictional story of *Lord of the Flies*, the United States began to openly tolerate practices that heretofore were considered illegal, unethical, or immoral. Examples of these practices include detaining people in a legal limbo, questioning when torture may be utilized, and the development of vigilante groups such as the "minute men" to patrol the Mexican border for illegal immigrants.

However, work organizations have always struggled to manage in the face of disruptions of all types. Let us begin by developing an understanding of some key terms. To do so, one can go to the *Disaster Response Journal* Web site (www.drj.com) and find the following definitions:

■ A **business interruption** is "any event, whether anticipated (i.e., public service strike) or unanticipated (i.e., blackout) which disrupts the normal course of business operations at an organization location."[5]

- **Business continuity planning** is a "process of developing advance arrangements and procedures that enable an organization to respond to an event in such a manner that critical business functions continue with planned levels of interruption or essential change."[6]
- **A business continuity program** is "an ongoing program supported and funded by executive staff to ensure business continuity requirements are assessed, resources are allocated, and recovery and continuity strategies and procedures are completed and tested."[7]
- **Business impact analysis (BIA)** is "the process of analyzing all business functions and the effect that a specific disaster may have upon them. Determining the type or scope of difficulty caused to an organization should a potential event identified by the risk analysis actually occur. The BIA should quantify, where possible, the loss impact from both a business interruption (number of days) and a financial standpoint."[8]

While some might differentiate between business continuity and a disaster response plan, for the purposes here, this will not be the case as these two terms seem to have a fair amount of redundancy. Further, as will become clearer, this author views a *disaster* as one type of business interruption, different from other types, yet on a continuum, an incident that must be addressed as part of a business continuity plan.

In 1994, this author wrote *Critical Incident Stress and Trauma in the Workplace.*[9] This book was written prior to Y2K, 9/11, the Murrah Building, and most of the worldwide upheavals. Its primary focus was responding to incidents that impact the workplace and in it was delineated the **categories** of events that remain relevant for this discussion:

- *Crisis:* "An interruption from a previously normal state of functioning resulting in turmoil, instability, and a significant upheaval to a system."[10] In this context, crises usually do not involve death or injury to personnel. Examples of crises would include layoffs, reorganizations, power outages, etc.
- *Trauma:* "An injury to living tissue caused by an extrinsic source. It may be the result of surgery, an act of violence, a natural disaster. Trauma usually results in a state of crisis."[11] In this context, trauma is not used to refer to emotional trauma, but rather when people are physically injured or killed. Examples might include an explosion, accident, violence, etc.
- *Disaster:* "Is a crisis in which there has been traumatic injury/death to many people often accompanied by destruction of property."[12] Examples would be transportation accidents, localized fires, etc.

- *Catastrophe*: Since the book was completed in 1994, *catastrophe* was added to the list to delineate those types of disasters that affect the infrastructure of the community. The difference between a disaster and a catastrophe is that one can remove oneself from the disaster, but cannot do so from the catastrophe. As an example, there might be a car accident involving six cars. There might be as many as eight to twelve victims with a wide range of traumatic injuries. This would be considered a disaster for the paramedics and emergency medical technicians (EMTs), as well as the pedestrian bystanders. However, one can leave the scene of the accident and return to a degree of normalcy. On the other hand, a flood or earthquake would be considered a catastrophe because it is difficult to remove oneself from the trauma and turmoil. The utilities are down, roads and communications systems are disrupted, and often the people who are providing services are impacted by the incident as well as the victims for whom they are caring.

Over time, other types of occurrences required further description, and **grief/bereavement** was added to the list to describe the deaths of employees that occur outside the workplace and are not witnessed by employees, yet may have a significant impact on operational continuity. It is the contention of this author that all disruptive events that impact any type of group or organization can be placed into one of the aforementioned categories. As discussed later, a pre-plan strategy for the wide range of events that might affect a workplace is an indispensable component to any response plan. Certainly, each **category** requires a more comprehensive and in-depth analysis and the development of subcategories within, which are discussed later in this section.

Table 2.1 is a list of incidents that might befall any work organization and impact its business continuity.[13] This list was taken with modification from Contingency Planning and Management (www.contingencyplanning.com), a worthwhile site for the reader to visit; and, while some of the events may have redundancy, it is a worthwhile exercise to go through to determine what type of incident might befall their workplace. Further, many of the types of incidents would have a very different impact were they to occur while people were at work versus if they were not in the workplace. Also, as discussed earlier, these are the types of events that can dramatically shift an organization's belief system and thus its culture.

To simplify this list, Table 2.2 breaks it down into five "types" of incidents that might befall a workplace causing disruption.

As one can imagine, each type brings with it its own unique set of circumstances and impacts on operations and personnel. Chapter 3 will provide an orientation toward assessing the incident and the potential consequence.

TABLE 2.1 Incidents That May Impact a Work Organization

Biological hazards	Loss of records
Blackouts	Medical emergencies
Business relocation	Mergers and acquisitions
Civil/community unrest	Negative publicity
Computer failure	Power outages
Computer viruses	Reduction in workforce
Computer hacking	Sick building syndrome
Delivery malfunctions	Staffing issues
Earthquakes	Succession planning
Electrical storms	Tornadoes
Environmental hazards	Transportation disruptions
Espionage	Unauthorized access
Fire	Virus attacks
Flooding	White collar crime
Hurricanes	Winter storms
Labor disputes	Workplace violence
Legal problems	

TABLE 2.2 Types of Business Disruption Incidents

Acts of Nature	Man-made I & II
Floods	Fires
Tornadoes	Hazardous materials
Hurricanes	Explosion
Earthquakes	Sabotage
Wild fires	Disruptive individual
Storms/blizzards	Violence
Other	Civil disorder
	Bomb threat, etc.
	Terrorist activity
Infrastructure Disruption	**Organizational Disruption**
Widespread power outage	Layoff
Water/sewerage system breakdown	Reorganization
Telecommunication outage	Buy/sell
Major computer system disruption	Relocation
	Strike, work stoppage
	Major change in policies, benefits

References

1. F. Capra, *The Hidden Connections,* Anchor Books, New York, 2004.
2. F. Capra, *The Hidden Connections,* Anchor Books, New York, 2004, p. 105.
3. F. Capra, *The Hidden Connections,* Anchor Books, New York, 2004, p. 105.
4. F. Capra, *The Hidden Connections,* Anchor Books, New York, 2004, p. 105.
5. *Disaster Response Journal,* Web site at www.drj.com.
6. *Disaster Response Journal,* Web site at www.drj.com.
7. *Disaster Response Journal,* Web site at www.drj.com.
8. *Disaster Response Journal,* Web site at www.drj.com.
9. G. Lewis, *Critical Incident Stress and Trauma in the Workplace,* Taylor & Francis, Philadelphia, 1994.
10. G. Lewis, *Critical Incident Stress and Trauma in the Workplace,* Taylor & Francis, Philadelphia, 1994.
11. G. Lewis, *Critical Incident Stress and Trauma in the Workplace,* Taylor & Francis, Philadelphia, 1994.
12. G. Lewis, *Critical Incident Stress and Trauma in the Workplace,* Taylor & Francis, Philadelphia, 1994.
13. Contingency Planning and Management, Web site at www.contingencyplanning.com.

Chapter 3

Incident Assessment: Proactive versus Reactive Measures

It is well acknowledged that part of any crisis response plan should determine the relative likelihood of an event occurring, and then establish some pre-incident response guidelines.

In his book entitled *Crisis Management: Planning for the Inevitable,*[1] Steven Fink describes how to derive a crisis impact value (CIV) by asking five questions and subjectively rating them on a 1 to 10 scale (1 represents a low likelihood of occurrence or impact, and 10 represents a very high likelihood of occurrence or impact).

- Might the crisis intensify and if so, how fast?
- How observable is the crisis by outsiders such as media, regulatory agencies, or customers?
- How much does it interfere with operations?
- Is the company the victim or culprit of this crisis?
- How damaging is it to the bottom line (however one defines bottom line)?

Each incident, being (proactively) evaluated, would receive a rating from 1 to 50, which would then be divided by 5 for the CIV score, which gets plotted along the vertical axis of the Crisis Plotting Grid as shown in Figure 3.1.

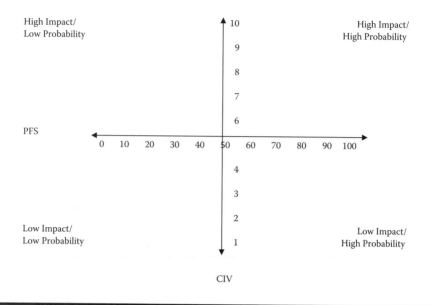

FIGURE 3.1   Sample of Fink's crisis plotting grid.

Next, Fink suggests deriving a Probability Factor Scale (PFS). Once again, this is a subjective rating that assesses the likelihood of an event occurring. This rating would be plotted on the horizontal axis of the Crisis Plotting Grid.

Fink then suggests that one can place different types of crises in the different quadrants and prioritize accordingly.

While this is an excellent exercise, it is my guess that many crisis/disaster/business continuity planners have already gone through similar types of exercises. However, my experience has been that most of these exercises do not really seem to assess the impact on personnel.

This chapter looks at assessing incidents and the potential social and emotional impacts on personnel. Previously, different categories of events (crisis, trauma, disaster, catastrophe, grief/bereavement) that might occur in the workplace were discussed. In addition, one must look at the five different types of events as described in Chapter 2: man-made I and II, natural disaster, organizational transition, infrastructure disruption. Each type is described briefly.

Man-Made I (Single Perpetrator)

Is an act of violence or hostility perpetrated by a single individual against an organization, its personnel, and its property? There may be death and destruction to a workgroup or a community that is the result of an individual, a group, or an act of nature. Taking either of the previous scenarios where four people were killed and many were injured in the hurricane or earthquake, let us now imagine that, instead of a natural act, it is the act of a lone gunman who walks into the workplace and begins to shoot randomly at people with the same result. The human reaction to either type of incident is extremely distressing; however, one can speculate that the tendency of people is to see acts of nature as just that and the reaction is usually one of grief, sadness, questioning of or returning to faith, etc. During incidents that involve acts of violence, there are often all of the aforementioned reactions. However, they also can be accompanied by anger, anxiety, apprehension about safety and security, etc. Further, the tendency is for the media to become more involved with the incident in a different way than if they were covering a storm or an earthquake. The incident tends to be covered for a longer time with media reporting diversifying into related areas of the story such as the perpetrator's family and childhood, as well as those of the victims, other incidents of similar events in other parts of the country, etc. There is often a profusion of "experts" giving 30-second sound bites of surface information that tends to do little more than exacerbate the anxiety.

During acts of nature, an entire geographic region might be affected, and people often bond together within communities. As the recovery effort evolves, people look to their local, state, and federal governments along with insurance companies to be "made whole." With man-made acts that occur within a specific work setting, there may be a sense of isolation from the community as people may feel some guilt by association. While family members and friends might reach out to the victims of a violent episode, it often feels like the world *keeps on goin'* while their world has stopped. It is often the legal system where many victims of these situations find themselves years later attempting to get some resolution. Unfortunately, the legal system tends to progress in a slow manner, and it can take years for a situation to be resolved. In Chapter 7, the legal and liability issues involved with crisis and trauma are discussed. Further, each stage of a legal proceeding brings with it "triggers" or associations to the original event, causing further disruptions.

Man-Made II (Organized Group)

Following along the same lines, when violence or hostility is perpetrated by an organized group, as in the case of terrorist action or gang-style violence, or violent protests, there is another layer added to the aforementioned reactions that involves a call for a political as well as a legal response. There may be a tendency for groups to split off into factions that are for or against a certain group. Politicians might use the events to gain political inroads. We have witnessed this in our country on numerous occasions in recent history. The events of 9/11, the Murrah Building, and Waco, Texas, are examples. We have witnessed the politicizing of these events… the tendency toward xenophobia… the increase in anxiety. All of this results in a change in the culture.

Organizational Transition

This is an event that has only affected an organization and has not spread beyond to involve the community. This may be a layoff, reorganization, strike, acquisition, relocation, etc. While there may be no damage, death, or injury to the employees or the workplace, there may certainly be a disruption in operations, continuity of business, and the concomitant emotional and social impact. Usually, there are rumors that run through an organization prior to any real event. These rumors, while perhaps maintaining a kernel of reality, often generate more anxiety and apprehension than minimizing the emotional distress.

Unfortunately, there is one type of transition that is quite widespread and causes a fair amount of organizational disruption. Further, it is the opinion of this author that many organizations handle this crisis quite poorly. I am referring to when a company must lay off a portion of its workforce. Vignette 3.1 is an article that this author wrote, describing the mismanagement and potential fallout of the, often customary, method of dismissing people from the workplace.

3.1 Layoffs for Cost… Not Cause: A Subtle Form of Workplace Hostility?

"Treat people with respect, you earn respect. Show them a guard and you have reasons to guard yourself. Hostility promotes hostility."

—Anonymous

Unfortunately, over the past couple decades, "workplace violence" has become a common term in our lexicon. Immediately, people begin to think of "disgruntled" employees coming into work with "guns ablazin'." As tragic and dramatic as these events are, the reality is that, in actuality, workplace homicides as well as non-fatal assaults have decreased significantly over the past decade. Further, co-worker–to–co-worker violence accounts for only about 10 percent of actual incidents.[1-3]

The data reported by the Bureau of Labor and Statistics indicates that the number of layoffs and the number of individuals affected by them have increased by more than 50 percent over the past eight years to more than 1 million "initial claimants for unemployment" per year.[4] While impacting potentially hundreds of thousands of individuals each year, it should be examined whether the method of termination that has become common practice (and perhaps well intended) might be considered discriminatory and perhaps a subtle form of hostile behavior on the part of the workplace.

While not all employers implement what this author calls the "show-them-the-door" method of termination, the scenario in many organizations may look something like this: the designated individuals are called into a conference room by a department head or supervisor, either one by one or as a group, and given a brief talk along with some forms or documents describing the terms of their discharge, benefits package, etc. Then the terminated employees are taken to their individual workstations, accompanied by a supervisor, security, or other type of monitoring personnel. They are assisted with the packing of their personal effects and then ushered out of the company with a clear suggestion not to return to the workplace. For many organizations, this has become the "justifiably" standard process. When asked why such a method is employed, the responses are usually vague references to security or protection of intellectual property. At other times, there may be an expressed concern about the laid-off employee(s) becoming a physical or emotional disruption to the workplace. Others indicate that seeing laid-off employees "moping" around the office might have a demoralizing impact on the remaining workers. Upon further reflection, one might liken this orientation of treating all individuals as if they were potential criminals or people with an emotional disturbance, to the practice of racial profiling (i.e., responding to or classifying an entire group of people on the basis of the behavior of a very small percentage of that group). It is as if an organization operates by the philosophy that "You were a good and trusted employee yesterday but because today we decided to terminate you... we don't trust you anymore and must treat you as a potential criminal."

Further, if the goal is to protect the other employees from the emotional turmoil of a layoff, one should question this methodology. Anecdotal information as well as research indicate that many employees feel great distress before, during, and after a layoff or reorganization. In his book entitled *Healing The Wounds*,[5] David Noer labels the people who *survive* a layoff as "survivor-victims," and describes their experience as akin, albeit on a lesser level, to people who survive trauma such as combat, the Holocaust, etc. They are left with feelings of survivor-guilt, anxiety about whether they will be next, hopelessness about the random nature of events, anger at the unfairness and seeming lack of purpose, etc. The surviving workers often become disorganized and demoralized, which diminishes their productivity. Further, there is often more tension and conflict among the remaining workforce. So, as an antidote to the demoralization of the remaining workers, this is a failed method. In fact, this author has heard people describe a "lack of closure" or "feeling the ghosts of the departed walking the halls" when their colleagues have been summarily dismissed.

The next question is whether the "show-them-the-door" method actually provides an increased level of security. "There's always going to be the person who thinks that 'If they let me go, I'm going to make them pay,'" warns a research manager of Internet Security Software. "If he knows the company is in trouble, he could plant a Trojan or leave some malicious time bomb that could go off when his name appears on a layoff list. There have been a number of cases of people doing just that."[6] Or, as another IT Director wrote: "To safeguard the company from possible retaliation, even when an effort is being made to treat the employee fairly, all access to company resources should be disabled promptly upon termination. Further, in most cases, the employee should be given a brief period to pack his or her things, then asked to vacate the facility on the same day of termination. This is especially true in the case of IT professionals."[7]

Although there is no "hard data" to support the incidents of malicious behavior that warrant this method, one can speculate that it might provide a certain degree of security as regards the employees who are being laid off at that moment. However, one should consider that it is equally possible that those who remain and bear witness to this type of treatment of their colleagues might be putting together their own "bailout" package, should the same experience befall them. Further, it has been clearly acknowledged that there is an increasing trend between layoffs and wrongful termination litigation, and the associated legal expense must be considered.[8, 9]

Perhaps one of the most extreme examples of the potential fallout is described in this excerpt from the *CIO* Web site:[10]

"I have been working in software development since the late 70's, and during this time I have seen my share of downsizing. Most of what I have seen has been done under what I would consider to be less than favorable conditions. In many cases, turning people who willingly would have taken a pay cut to keep their jobs into people who would stop at nothing to damage the company or its reputation. The most vivid memory comes from my time at Bell Labs. In this instance, the switching division decided that the factory in Mexico offered a cheaper product than the factory in North Carolina. So instead of doing any type of announcement and transition, AT&T chose to perform the layoff using the following fake fire alarm paradigm. The fire alarm went off and all of the employees were herded to the parking lot. After all of the employees were accounted for, the doors were all chained except one, and each employee was escorted to their work area to pick up any personal effects and given a 2-week severance check. Needless to say, this not only resulted in a large number of disgruntled ex-employees, but shook the morale and conscience of other employees of AT&T who were not affected by the immediate layoff."

As suggested in *How to Avoid Litigation from Layoffs*, "[e]mployees are less likely to sue if they are satisfied with their severance packages and you treat them with dignity and respect in the discharge process."[11]

In his book entitled *I Don't Want to Talk about It*, Terrance Real describes two different types of trauma: "active" and "passive." Put simply, active trauma is when we are hurt, be it physically or emotionally. Passive trauma is when, after being injured, we receive insufficient support, nurturance, or kindness. Or, in fact, when we are further injured by being shamed, rejected, or humiliated about the active trauma.[12] Examples to clarify how these two types of trauma interact are as follows. A child, injured during a Little League game, is reprimanded by his or her coach or parent about the error that was committed. Or, after surgery, a female cancer patient is rejected by her husband. Or, upon returning from combat, Viet Nam era soldiers were treated as "murderers." Or, finally, an employee who is told that he is losing his job/income/identity experiences further humiliation by the aforementioned method of separating people from the workplace.

While "reduction in force" has been common for many professional groups (e.g., construction, tourism, etc.), it now is being utilized in many work organizations. In his book entitled *The Future of Success*, Robert Reich, the former Secretary of Labor in the Clinton Administration, reported that it has been only in the last 20 to 30 years that employees have been laid off for cost (rather than cause) on the scale that is now seen.[13]

One might argue that this method, if not similar to profiling, is reactionary, possibly discriminatory, and is borne out of a shortsighted concern for security and liability rather than a viable and comprehensive plan. Further, many forward-thinking companies have discovered that it is not necessary to use this method when letting go employees for cost... not cause. And, in 1989 the Federal Government issued the Workers Adjustment and Retraining Notification Act (WARN). Briefly, "a covered employer must give notice if there is to be a mass layoff which does not result from a plant closing, but which will result in an employment loss at the employment site during any 30-day period for 500 or more employees, or for 50–499 employees if they make up at least 33% of the employer's active workforce. An employer who violates the WARN provisions by ordering a plant closing or mass layoff without providing appropriate notice is liable to each aggrieved employee for an amount including back pay and benefits for the period of violation, up to 60 days."[14] The Department of Labor continues on to suggest that "While this applies to large-scale layoffs, it sets the tone and priority that employees must be given ample notification of job loss. With the WARN provision implemented, what does this do to the aforementioned security concerns? One may speculate that there should be even greater concern if it is a large-scale downsizing with respect to the aforementioned issues of security. Why shouldn't the same priority be designated for smaller organizations or lesser numbers? It is therefore prudent for employers to weigh the desirability of advance notice against the possibility of expensive and time-consuming litigation to resolve disputes where notice has not been given. The Department encourages employers to give notice in all circumstances."[15]

When an organization is forced to downsize, it should be considered not just a fiscal crisis, but also an emotional one that impacts all involved. The long-range influence on the total organization extends well beyond the departure of the designated employees. "Managing transition during organizational downsizing often means guiding employees through the 'survivor syndrome' — a post-traumatic disorder linked to survivors of major crisis situations. In order to avert the survivor syndrome, remaining employees must feel they are valued by management. Survivors tend to react more favorably when they believe that downsizing is being handled fairly. It is up to management to maintain that perception of fairness during times of transition. Providing employees with reasons for downsizing helps solidify trust between employees and management. Open and frank discussion is also crucial.... All affected individuals should be notified well in advance."[16]

Recommendations:

It goes without saying (but it must be said nonetheless), being laid off as a result of a downsizing or reorganization is an extremely stressful event for all involved. Certainly, for the employees who are being "let go," there may be far-reaching financial, familial, and emotional reactions for them as well as their family members. It has been noted that a percentage of people demonstrate a wide range of reactions to losing their jobs, including anger, shame, anxiety, depression, addictions, and self- and other-directed hostility. Even for those not acutely impacted, the long-term stress of unemployment and the financial and relational difficulties that it may spawn can impact an entire family. Therefore, the following are some recommendations that may mitigate the impact for all employees.

- Do not notify people on a Friday that they are being laid off. The weekend is a time when unemployment offices are not open, and other opportunities to find jobs, headhunters, resume services, etc. are unavailable.
- Preferably, the holiday season is not the best time to deprive people of their incomes. Yet, so often, work organizations choose this time due to the schedule of their fiscal calendar.
- Let people know on Monday, Tuesday, or Wednesday of the week. If they choose, allow them to come back to the office for the remainder of the week to pack their belongings, say their goodbyes, etc.
- An informal brunch or luncheon for the affected department(s) may be of benefit.
- Allow the individuals to use their offices (or a designated location) for outplacement services. Provide computers, copy machines, fax machines, and Internet access for personnel to look for employment.

- Provide outplacement services for the affected employees.
- Have the EAP available to people for a month after their leave the company.
- Have the EAP or another facilitator conduct small group debriefings for the remaining employees to discuss how this has impacted them.
- Train the supervisors and department heads in how to deal with the transition. Provide consultation and training to supervisors of departments that have been affected by the cuts around personnel management strategies. As David Gershaw writes in his article, "Surviving a Layoff," "When any transition occurs, supervisors' support of the workers is a critical factor. Workers need to have supervisors who are willing to listen and provide both emotional and practical support. When this occurs, both job performance and commitment to the organization among the workers are higher. If companies want the commitment of their employees, it would help to train their supervisors to provide support for the workers."[18] Practice the five "As" of organizational recovery:
  - **Attitude:** be open, honest, and straightforward.
  - **Awareness** of employees reactions.
  - **Acknowledge** the event and allow for the expression of reactions.
  - **Availability:** have supervisors and departments be highly visible.
  - **Appreciation:** express appreciation to all employees.

References

1. NIOSH, Violence in the Workplace: Homicide in the Workplace, retrieved May 30, 2003, from http://www.cdc.gov/niosh/violhomi.html.
2. Bureau of Justice Statistics (BJS), Violence in the Workplace, 1993–99, U.S. Department of Justice, Washington, D.C., December 2001.
3. Bureau of Labor Statistics (BLS), BLS Survey of Occupational Injuries and Illnesses, Department of Labor, Washington D.C., November 2002.
4. Bureau of Labor and Statistics as reported in http://stats.bls.gov/news.release/mmls.toc.htm.
5. D. Noer, *Healing the Wounds; Overcoming the Trauma of Layoffs,* Jossey-Bass, San Francisco, 1993.
6. Taken from Corporate Layoffs Create Security Havoc for IT Pros, July 2, 2002, www.itmanagement.earthweb.com/secu/article.php/1380141.
7. Taken from Corporate Layoffs Create Security Havoc for IT Pros, July 2, 2002, www.itmanagement.earthweb.com/secu/article.php/1380141.
8. B. Guryen, Careful Planning Can Reduce Litigation Risk in Layoffs, *The Journal of New England Technology,* April 15–19, 2001, Vol. 19, No. 15., www.masshightech.com.
9. Current Litigation Glut Outcome of Early 90s Layoffs, taken from www.cutter.com/research/1998/crb980716.html.
10. Taken from www.cio.com.
11. Taken from www.lfhc.com/layoffs.cfm.
12. T. Real, *I Don't Want to Talk about It,* Scribner, New York, 1997.
13. R. Reich, *The Future of Success,* Alfred A. Knopf, New York, 2000.

14. Taken from www.dol.gov.
15. Taken from www.dol.gov/dol/allcfr/ETA/Title_20/Part_639/20CFR639.1.htm.
16. Taken from www.rcmp-learning.org/docs/ecdd0058.htm.
17. Taken from www.azwestern.edu/psy/dgershaw/lol/Layoff.html.

In *Psychopathology in the Workplace,* Jay Thomas and Mandy Davies wrote in their chapter, entitled "Stress, Working Conditions and Work-Life Events" that while mergers, acquisitions, and downsizing are quite common, they are often characterized with "high turnover, low morale, low satisfaction and commitment, unproductive behavior, sabotage, absenteeism and negative employee attitudes and behaviors."[2] They go on to report that research indicates that anxiety for remaining employees after a layoff is stimulated as they "face fewer resources, more workload demands, and uncertainty regarding their future employment."[3] Further, the culture undergoes a dramatic shift and it often takes several years for new values to emerge and gel into a new culture.

During these times, significant efforts must be made to:

- Provide as much factual information as possible to all employees. "Employees need both useful information regarding coming changes and frequent communication to develop positive attitudes and trust for the new management."[4]
- Nurture the new corporate identity to help foster a sense of belonging.
- Clarify role changes within the organization.
- Acknowledge shifts in goals and values for the new organization.

The preceding was a brief description of the general types of events that might befall a workplace and some of the ensuing dynamics that can develop. To truly assess the impact on personnel, each of these types of events must also be assessed, looking at ten factors that could determine a very different impact on personnel and thus require a different level of emotional response. The ten factors to consider are discussed below.

Factor 1: Locus of Impact

When an incident does occur, there should be contingencies dependent upon the area of impact. A fire, power outage, or flood might just affect a specific area of an organization. Or, just as likely, it could impact the entire building or geographic region. Therefore, any pre-incident assessment should look at and plan for a response relative to the locus of impact.

Part of Building

If a portion of a work environment is impacted by a business disruption event, it might result only in the closing of that one area of operation. Activities in other areas or departments might carry on unaffected, or might be influenced by the event as well. Questions — such as how much downtime will transpire; what to do with the personnel; can they and their duties and responsibilities be temporarily transferred to another area of operation — must be assessed. If there is to be a transfer of personnel, it must be evaluated just how this will impact the "transferees," their families, as well as the department or work area into which they are being transferred.

Total Facility

The same questions must be addressed; however, a total business shutdown is usually a much more dramatic event, requiring a greater level of intervention. Certainly, the primary focus is on getting the work operations back on line. However, if people are being released from work, this can result in transportation issues, pay status for the time out, etc. Imagine that people are being released from work as a result of discovering Anthrax, as was the case with the U.S. Postal Service (USPS) building in Washington, D.C.; or as a result of a power outage due to overloaded circuits; or due to a fire. In the case of the power outage, the people might return to work in a relatively short period of time with little to no apparent signs of damage. With the fire, it might take a longer time or people might be temporarily displaced while their area is rehabbed. In the case of the U.S. Postal Service, people were out for two years and had been transferred to other locations. During that extended time period, people developed new relationships and workgroups. Some preferred their "temporary" placement to their original placement. There was a much higher level of apprehension and adjustment when the time came to return to their original worksite. (It should be noted that the USPS devoted much time and resources to planning the return and reentry to the original building.) With the example of a fire, safety was the primary concern, as was discovering how the fire started and what efforts were made to ensure that it would not happen again. With the Anthrax, safety and security were both primary priorities. Because it was a man-made event and the perpetrators never found, it resulted in a heightened sense of ongoing concern. Further, the original event resulted in the death of two workers, leaving all feeling vulnerable. With the power outage, it was about how to protect the technology and the personnel issues were of lesser concern.

As these examples point out, the planner must look at all factors involved with any incident and predict the possible emotional repercussions.

Local/Regional Area

Should a city or local geographic area be affected, all of the aforementioned factors must be taken into account. However, one additional critical factor is involved with an incident of this level: families of the workers are impacted by the incident. Schools in the area might be closed or releasing children, roads and utilities might be impaired, and spouses might be trying to reach each other with limited modes of communication available to them. Elderly parents may be in need of assistance from their working children. People might be displaced from their homes to temporary shelters or living with relatives. Daycare and schools might be closed; social service and healthcare agencies might be overwhelmed. Family members might be called upon to provide services to others. Often, a work environment can be returned to some level of work stability and productivity before the workers' personal environment.

It should be noted that with these types of events, certain professions or certain workers within professions might be considered "essential," "critical," or "key." For example, utility workers and police, fire, and hospital personnel may need to stay on the job while others are being sent home. What has been noted is that special care must be devoted to these groups. The following anecdote will clarify some of the issues. This story was told to the author by an attendee at one of his workshops about the recovery efforts during and after Hurricane Andrew. During that time there was extensive damage to property as well as utilities and roadways. The public service workers were informed that they needed to stay on the job to restore power and clear roadways. However, the workers were also hearing stories of flooding as well as looting in certain areas. They were willing to work but felt a terrific sense of role conflict; who do they take care of... their job or their families and homes? There were some struggles before it was acknowledged that people needed to take care of their personal priorities before they could focus on professional ones.

What should also be mentioned is that with incidents of this magnitude, there may be a state or regional emergency management response that, from a social/emotional perspective, creates another whole set of dynamics and issues. While the "calling out" agencies provide needed support and acknowledge the level of the incident, they also may generate a certain degree of anxiety and apprehension. Factors such as declared states of emergency, curfews, media coverage, Red Cross, National Guard, politicians, etc. might inadvertently escalate the emotional situation for individuals, families, communities, work organizations, as well as politicians.

Factor 2: Timing

Suddenness versus Warning

Regardless of the type of incident (man-made, natural disaster, organizational transition, infrastructure disruption), one of the critical factors that influences potential human reactions, as well as organizational response strategy, is whether or not there is any warning prior to the event. One concept generally acknowledged about human behavior is that if there is time to plan and prepare, to organize and implement, then people tend to have a greater capacity to manage the incident. When this author conducts training programs, I ask the audience to consider two scenarios and to speculate about the reactions of the individuals involved. Both of these events have resulted in significant damage to property and infrastructure, as well as four deaths and multiple injuries. People have been displaced, schools and businesses as well as some major roadways have been closed. From an objective paradigm, both have caused equal tragedy. However, one event was a hurricane with subsequent flooding that had been predicted for several days prior to the onset. The other was a moderate earthquake that came suddenly and without warning. The earthquake occurred mid-morning when people were at work or home and children at school. In the case of the hurricane, one can speculate that people had a pre-impact phase that allowed them to prepare for the event. Gathering family members together, covering windows, stocking in foods, or evacuating, allows for a sense of preparedness and thus a greater sense of personal control. In the other situation, the earthquake struck without warning or preparedness. Family members may not know of the status of others and may be unable to reach them by phone or road. It is a time of chaos and confusion. Let us leave these scenarios and explore further the impact of other factors.

Factor 3: Duration

Ongoing versus Contained

Once again, referencing the aforementioned scenarios, in the case of the hurricane, it is an ongoing event with a pre-impact, impact, and post-impact stage. While people might have had a chance to prepare for the hurricane by boarding up their homes, evacuating the area, stocking in supplies, and gathering family together, the event is considered ongoing in that it does not have a clear end. Even after the hurricane has passed, the flooding may continue for some time, wreaking further havoc and continuing to cause even more damage. Efforts to repair and rebuild must wait until floodwaters recede and roads reopen before recovery can actually begin. On the other hand, while the earthquake may have been initially much more disruptive and emotionally devastating as it caught people off-guard, it is over (contained) and people and organizations can immediately assess the damage and begin to bring resources to bear.

Another way to look at this continuum is to decide whether the situation has stabilized or if there is potential for continued escalation resulting in further damage. Just because an incident is considered contained or over does not mean to imply that the emotional devastation is over. In fact, for many situations, it is not until the incident is contained that the emotional impact is experienced. Any incident has an ongoing quality to it even when it may be over. As an example, many readers might remember the Station Club fire in Rhode Island in which 100 people were killed and many sustained serious burns and injuries. While this event was considered "contained," as it was limited to a specific building and the fire was put out within hours, the repercussions of the incident continued to escalate for many weeks, and the ripple effect continued on for months and years. A later chapter discusses the life cycle of a crisis or disaster and the ripple effect that continues to play out long after an event has ended.

Factor 4: Impact on Operations

This is the typical focus of the BIA that most organizations are accustomed to performing. It focuses on the impact on the operations of an organization. Do operations come to a complete stop, or is it a manageable disruption? Because most readers are familiar with this type of analysis, space will not be devoted to describing this factor.

Factors 5 through 9: Damage and Injury

While an impact analysis might focus on the impact of an incident on business operations, often it does not include looking beyond the four walls (be they virtual or otherwise) of an organization. Business property, operations, and security are certainly a critical priority but may be easier to assess and restore than the damage to personnel or personal property, business reputation, and the resulting impact of these factors on operations.

Factor 5: Damage to Premises

Has the workplace itself sustained a significant amount of damage? Fires, floods, and violence often leave the workplace in a state of structural disruption. Time is necessary to rebuild and rehab the facilities. Often, this can result in the relocation of personnel or operations. Chapter 6 describes this factor in greater detail.

Factor 6: Damage to Reputation

Another "damage" issue discussed in greater detail in a later chapter is the potential liability to the organization as well as the damage to its reputation. While many incidents such as floods or hurricanes are akin to "no-fault" incidents, the "man-made" or "organizational" incidents such as violence, layoffs, strikes, and harassment claims can cause significant operational disruption while also resulting in damage to the organization's reputation... which can then cause further operational as well as personnel disruption.

Factor 7: Injury and Death to Personnel

As will be discussed at another point, it is the opinion of this author that the death of workers while on the job must be handled as a top priority with certain specific interventions. Acknowledgment of the death of employees while at work takes precedence even above that of restoration of operations. Usually, this is the case; however, there are organizations that tend to see the restoration of operations as the main concern and the on-site death of its personnel as a lesser matter. Of course, in certain professions such as public safety, government, military, medical, etc., operations must continue even in the face of line-of-duty death and serious injury.

Factor 8: Personal Property

When the author first began writing this book, the state of Florida had been hit by three devastating hurricanes within one month. The financial toll was in the billions. There had been numerous deaths, displacement, and destruction of property. The federal and state emergency management teams had been involved, along with the Red Cross, National Guard, U.S. Coast Guard, and other support agencies. While businesses focused on resumption of operations, this was usually completed in a relatively short amount of time. However, in these situations, many of the employees continued to experience the ongoing impact of the hurricane on a personal level for a much greater duration in the form of:

- Temporary dislocation from homes
- Damage to personal property (homes, cars, recreational vehicles and boats)
- Resolving insurance claims and the subsequent premium increase
- Destruction of personal and sentimental valuables
- Emotional disruption to children as well as family pets (yes, do not forget them)
- Disorganization to the social community
- Debris and garbage visible for weeks
- Children being bused to different schools
- Religious buildings damaged
- Stores closed
- ATM machines not working
- Neighbors permanently relocating

It may be weeks or months before the social community is restored to a semblance of normalcy.

Factor 9: Impact on and Damage to Social Structure

While many crises might not cause death, damage, or destruction beyond a specific area, there are situations in which the social structure can be impacted. Drawing on 9/11 as a dramatic example, there was little damage and destruction beyond lower Manhattan; however, the social structure in the surrounding communities was severely affected as many residents who worked in the towers had been killed or injured. Still others knew of victims of or lost family members. In a similar manner, the Station Club fire in Rhode Island in which 100 people were killed was a contained incident, and yet communities from all over Rhode Island and Massachusetts remain affected years later.

Factor 10: Concurrent Stressors

Whether it is humans or work organizations, stress is considered cumulative. As discussed previously, premorbid history and toxicity are factors that can exacerbate the reaction to a significant event, even if they seem unrelated. Issues that might raise an organization's toxicity — such as labor management relationships, financial stability, recent changes in demographics, etc. — are considered concurrent stressors. If an organization is under a lot of stress and is then hit by a crisis, it can result in a stronger reaction on the part of personnel or an exacerbation of the pre-incident stressors.

The Human Impact Assessment Tool (HIAT)

This author has developed an assessment "tool" that might enable a planner to *think* about the social and emotional impacts on personnel. This is not a statistical instrument or an exact, scientifically derived measure, but rather a brief estimate of potential impact. Using this tool, rate each of the previously described factors on a 1 to 10 scale, with 10 being a high score. A total score of more than 50 should be considered an event that could generate significant stress on the workforce, thus requiring intervention strategies. The following are some examples of utilizing this tool for different kinds of incidents.

For the purposes of example, several incidents will be assessed, the first being September 11, 2001. This is a company with 1200 employees. It is a financial institution that relies heavily on technology and has satellite offices throughout the country. Some 850 of the employees are located in the corporate office, while the other 350 are in the satellite offices across the country. For the purposes of this exercise, concurrent stressors have been rated at a mid-range of 5. Also, this organization is located in Manhattan, approximately two blocks from Ground Zero

Table 3.1 shows the assessment tool utilized for the 9/11 event.

Points of Discussion:

- **Locus of impact** was rated as 8 because of the suddenness of the incident, and thus limited time to transfer operations or to even notify the satellite offices. Further, the entire city and, in fact, the region was affected by the event. However, within a day or so, operations were able to be transferred to remote sites or satellite offices.
- **Timing** was rated as 10 because the attack occurred without any warning, thus allowing no time to prepare, organize, or respond.
- **Duration.** While the incident was "over" within a few hours, it was considered unstable and, in fact, there was great worry about escalation of more events, bad air quality, etc. Therefore, along the contained versus uncontained perspective, it was considered ongoing and thus uncontained, resulting in a score of 10.
- **Impact on operations.** There was an immediate shutdown of operations and people were immediately evacuated. Although data was backed up and systems were in place within 24 to 48 hours, this was a substantial impact on operations, and thus a score of 10.
- **Injury and damage to premises.** People could not return to the building for a week, and operations had to be transferred to other

TABLE 3.1 The HIAT with 9/11

	Man-made I	Man-made II	Natural Disaster	Organizational Transition	Infrastructure Disruption
Locus of impact		8			
Timing		10			
Duration		10			
Impact on operations		10			
I/D premises		10			
I/D personnel		7			
I/D reputation		1			
I/D personal property		2			
I/D social system		7			
Concurrent stressors		5			
Total score		70			

Note: I/D is injury/damage.

locations. The offices had to be cleaned of dust and some debris. While there was not extensive damage to the office or building, specifically, the street, lobby and surrounding areas were dramatically effected. Thus a score of 10.

■ **Impact/injury and damage to personnel.** While no employees were killed or injured, people had to immediately evacuate the building and were witness to the trauma on the street. At the time, there was no immediate accounting of all personnel. It should be noted that one need not be a victim of an event to experience a traumatic reaction. As described in Chapter 4, when discussing post-traumatic stress disorder (PTSD), just witnessing the death or injury of others can dramatically affect an individual. (9/11 was rated as 7.)

■ **Impact/injury and damage to reputation.** While not the fault of the work organization, this type of event could have some impact on reputation. Thus a score of 1 was given.

■ **Impact/injury and damage to employee residences.** Some lived near Ground Zero and could not immediately return to their homes. A rating of 2.

■ **Impact and damage to social structure.** There was far-reaching impact to utilities, transportation, communication, etc. In addition, while few in this company were injured or killed, they knew of many others in their communities or workplace who did die or were seriously injured. Further, many witnessed the event as well as the immediate aftermath. A rating of 7.

A score of 70 indicates a significant impact on personnel.

Shooting Incident with Three Dead and Four Wounded

Table 3.2 shows the impact of a shooting incident using the assessment tool. An ex-employee, who had been terminated for cause three months earlier, entered the building and randomly shot at employees as he walked through the office. While stopping to reload, he was tackled by several employees and restrained until the police arrived. The company is located on three floors and this happened in one area on one floor. The other two floors were unaware of the incident until it was over and the police were sweeping all offices. Many employees on the affected floor evacuated the building, and there was no organized system to account for all employees or visitors. At the reception desk, the sign-in document indicates that there were 28 visitors on company premises at the time of the incident.

TABLE 3.2 The HIAT with Shooting Incident

	Man-made I	Man-made II	Natural Disaster	Organizational Transition	Infrastructure Disruption
Locus of impact	5				
Timing	10				
Duration	6				
Impact on operations	8				
I/D premises	10				
I/D personnel	10				
I/D reputation	7				
I/D personal property	0				
I/D social system	1				
Concurrent stressors	5				
Total score	62				

Note: I/D is injury/damage.

Points of Discussion:

- **Locus of impact** was limited to the workplace facility. While this type of an event is certainly tragic and rather devastating, people can leave and return to their homes and support systems, which have not been affected by the incident. Thus, this factor was scored as 5.
- **Timing.** As there was no warning, this was rated as 10.
- **Duration.** The incident was over within 20 minutes, but there is significant ongoing impact. Law enforcement is still investigating. People are being interviewed. The media is highly visible and intrusive. Further, the office will be closed "until further notice." Thus a rating of 6.
- **Impact on operations.** The incident immediately shut down operations for at least one week in the corporate building; however, there was some ability to transfer operations to other locations. After the first week, only a skeletal staff was allowed into the building to facilitate operations. Thus a score of 8.
- **Damage to premises** was extensive, with much blood and gore. In addition, it was a crime scene and could not be disturbed until the investigation was complete. Further, efforts were to be made to rehab and reconfigure the office space, which would require relocation to another temporary space. Thus a rating of 10.
- **Injury and damage to personnel.** With employees being killed or injured, this was rated as 10.
- Injury/damage to residence is limited (rating 0).
- **Injury and damage to reputation** was determined as 7 because often after these types of events, the organization experiences a negative impact from the public and customers.
- **Social structure** was not impacted, except for those employees; rating of 1.
- **Concurrent stressors,** as stated, a rating of 5.

A total score of 62 and thus the expectation is that this event could certainly have a dramatic impact on personnel.

Power Outage

There is a major power outage similar to the one that occurred in the northeast region of the United States in 2003. It lasted for about six hours and resulted in people being released from work. Transportation and utilities were down for the time. Many people stayed within the city

TABLE 3.3   The HIAT with Power Outage

	Man-made I	Man-made II	Natural Disaster	Organizational Transition	Infrastructure Disruption
Locus of impact					8
Timing					10
Duration					3
Impact on operations					5
I/D premises					2
I/D personnel					2
I/D reputation					3
I/D personal property					2
I/D social system					3
Concurrent stressors					5
Total score					43

Note: I/D is injury/damage.

because there was no way to drive to their homes in the suburbs. Schools had to stay open to manage the children until parents could make arrangements to pick them up. Hospitals ran on emergency generators. There were some reports of looting and robberies but, in general, things remained calm for the duration. State emergency management organizations were activated. Table 3.3 shows the assessment of this type of incident utilizing the HIAT.

Points of Discussion:

- **Locus of impact** was 8, as this was a major power outage that affected a large geographic area.
- **Timing.** There was no warning, thus a score of 10.
- **Duration** was scored as 3, as the outage was over in a relatively short period of time with limited "ripple effect."
- **Impact on operations** was scored as 5. While there was some fallout from customers, much of the work was backed up and not lost.
- **Injury/damage to premises** was rated as 2.
- **Injury/damage to personnel** was rated as 2, as some people were trapped in the building and commuting home was a significant problem. Some were unable to pick up their children at school or daycare.
- **Injury/damage to reputation** was rated as 3. There were some complaints from customers who were unable to do business for a while.
- **Injury/damage to residence** was rated as a 2. Some people experienced loss of food as a result of refrigerators and freezers defrosting. There was other minor damage to other residences.
- **Damage to social structure** was rated as 3. Utilities and communication systems were down for 12 to 24 hours in some locations. ATMs and other services were disrupted.
- **Concurrent stressors** was rated as 5.

The total score was 43. This suggests a minimal social and emotional impact on the total workforce.

Major Hurricane

A large, individual hurricane similar in scope to those in September 2004 (Frances, Charley, and Ivan) hits the coast of Florida at about 7 p.m. The company is located approximately two miles inland, off a major highway.

TABLE 3.4 The HIAT with Hurricane

	Man-made I	Man-made II	Natural Disaster	Organizational Transition	Infrastructure Disruption
Locus of impact			10		
Timing			2		
Duration			8		
Impact on operations			6		
I/D premises			5		
I/D personnel			1		
I/D reputation			1		
I/D personal property			8		
I/D social system			9		
Concurrent stressors			5		
Total score			55		

Note: I/D is injury/damage.

Employees live in the surrounding areas, with many living closer to the coast. Table 3.4 represents an evaluation of this incident utilizing the HIAT.

Once again, it must be stated that this is neither an exact science nor a clinical or technological assessment, but rather a tool to facilitate thinking about the potential impact on personnel.

Points of Discussion:

Once again, the locus of impact was rated very high as this was a large-scale natural disaster that affected an entire region. The hurricane had been forecast for several days, thus allowing for emergency management planning, evacuation, etc. Between the pre-incident planning, the hurricane itself and the following flooding, etc, it was considered as having a long duration. Business functions were significantly impacted by the experience but did not totally shut down operations as some work was shifted to other facilities outside the region. There was limited damage to the building itself and the reputation of the organization. Employees experienced a significant amount of damage to personal property and their homes. The social structure of the region was considerably affected by the hurricane with loss of power, utilities, transportation, etc.

A subjective score of 55 indicates that there could be a noteworthy social and emotional impact on employees that should be planned for and managed.

References

1. Fink, Steven. *Crisis Management: Planning for the Inevitable,* iUniverse, Inc., Lincoln, NE, 2002.
2. J. Thomas and M. Davies, Stress, Working Conditions and Work-Life Events, in *Psychopathology in the Workplace*, Brunner-Rutledge, New York, 2004.
3. I. Nikandrou, N. Papalexandris, and D. Bourantas, D., Gaining Employee Trust after Acquisition: Implications for Managerial Action, *Employee Relations,* 24, 334–355, 2000.
4. J. Astrachan, Organizational Departures: The Impact of Separation Anxiety as Studied in Mergers and Acquisition Simulations, *Journal of Applied Behavioral Sciences*, 31, 31–50, 1995.

Chapter 4

Reactions to Crises, Traumas, Disasters, Catastrophes

This chapter discusses the potential psychological impacts on the individual, family, and work organization. The focus is to familiarize readers with key diagnostic labels and the symptomatology of each. In addition, readers will understand the impact on the individual, his or her family, and the work organization.

Stress

What is all the stress about stress? Initially, Hans Selye, known as the "Father of Stress," wrote extensively on the topic of stress.[1] Since then, books and articles on stress have found their way to such diverse outlets as *The Wall Street Journal* and *The Christian Science Monitor*, the *Journal of the American Medical Association,* and numerous other professional journals. The past several decades have seen the concept of stress grow to become a regular product of the media, marketing, as well as manufacturing. Books, tapes, and videos are available that purport to reduce stress or at least help individuals manage it. "Alternative health," the term that now encompasses interventions such as biofeedback, meditation, herbal remedies, acupuncture, aromatherapy, massage, reflexology, and spiritual workshops has grown from the activities of small groups to a mainstream staple. In the mid-1970s, Herbert Benson wrote *The Relaxation Response,*[2] in which he proposed that the people who practiced transcendental meditation had lower blood pressure and lived healthier lives. Further, he proposed that he could simulate the same biological response by teaching people a simple form of relaxation exercise. Using measures of heart rate, blood pressure, and galvanic skin measurements, his theory was proven correct. Benson, a cardiologist, became a major influence in the alternative health movement, writing several books about the practice of meditation, prayer, and other forms of healing. Since then, universities and medical centers such as UMASS Medical Center have developed Mind-Body Departments that research and provide courses and programs on alternative forms of health.

If one googles the term "workplace stress" or "stress in the workplace," one will get more than 1, 300,000 sites. Simply stated, stress is "an adaptive response, moderated by individual differences, that is a consequence of any action, situation, or event that places special demands on a person."[3] Taking the concept to a more comprehensive level, a stressful event can be assessed by determining three factors: (1) importance, (2) uncertainty, and (3) duration. *Importance* refers to "how significant the event is to the individual." *Uncertainty* refers to the lack of clarity about the outcome of the event. And *duration* refers to the time factor involved. While there are many other determinants for causing stress, these three can be considered the basic building blocks of stress.

It should be understood that stress is everywhere... and that it is not all bad. In the 1960s, Holmes and Raye developed the Social Readjustment Rating Scale,[4] a list of lifetime events with "stress points" assigned to each. People taking this questionnaire could then determine what level of stress they had experienced during the past year. Included were events that were considered negative: jail, divorce, death of a spouse, loss of job. However, also included were positive events such as retirement, vacation, Christmas. While this scale is often referred to in the stress literature, it has come under scrutiny and question as to whether it is a true instrument by which to measure stress. Further, it is a bit outdated (e.g., mortgage of $10,000 or more). Also, each item must be interpreted by the individual. For example, "change in living conditions" or "business readjustment" could be a move to a better residence or an increase or decrease in the work situation. Change in work responsibilities could be positive or negative. The point is that any change is considered stressful, as it is just that... a change from the usual and customary.

In September 2004, *The New York Times* ran a three-segment overview on stress and its impact on the workplace entitled "Sick of Work" by John

Schwartz.[5] He describes the changes in the work culture with its boundaries blurred by technology, lack of security, ailing pension plans, and diminishing benefits. Citing international studies, he explained that Americans work, on average, 1800 hours per year, which is more than the Germans and Japanese (both groups thought of as workaholic cultures). Schwartz referenced studies indicating that many workers feel that their work had increased in the past six months and that they do not use all of their allotted vacation time. Further, citing studies from Europe as well as the United States, indications are that employees experience a significant risk to their health when the work organization goes through a downsizing; however, there is an even greater risk to health when the company goes through an expansion. And finally, the article describes the relationship between work stress and the development of other problems, such as sleep deprivation, overeating, or drinking and the impact on family life. It should be noted that for many workers this is the usual and customary lifestyle of the modern worker. Add to that a crisis or traumatic incident in the workplace and it may function as the last straw on the overtaxed camel's back.

Beyond Stress

While stress is considered a normal part of life and many people manage the stress in their lives with limited negative impact, growing evidence suggests that there is a continuum between stress and more serious emotional conditions and mental disorders. Further, individuals have varying abilities and levels of resilience, and thus have different reactions to the impact. It has been determined that a high level of stress that goes on for a long duration may lead to an elevated level of physical, emotional, and cognitive impairment. As a colleague of this author once stated (and he may have heard it from someone else), "It's not the stress that gets you... it's the strain." "Estimates and projections from government, industry, and health groups place the cost of stress at approximately 150 billion dollars annually."[6] Some of this is the result of accidents and injuries, an increase in healthcare claims, visits to physicians, and other factors. As indicated in the aforementioned *New York Times* article, figures often cited are as high as $300 billion per year.

As the field of behavioral health has developed and the stigma surrounding the receipt of psychological services has diminished, there is a growing awareness that one does not have to be "crazy" to experience significant emotional difficulties. In fact, it is estimated that depression and anxiety disorder are affecting greater numbers of people. The National

Mental Health Association (NMHA) reports a wide range of statistics on its Web site; the following is a representative sample of recent data on depression, which estimates that:

- Approximately 18.8 million American adults, or about 9.5 percent of the U.S. population age 18 and older in a given year, have a depressive disorder.
- American employees used about 8.8 million sick days in 2001 due to untreated or mistreated depression. Employee absenteeism due to depression cost U.S. businesses between $33 billion and $44 billion per year. (NCQA, Sept. 2002; NIMA)
- In a typical workplace with twenty employees, four will likely develop a mental illness this year.[7]

The two major disorders that seem connected to the stress of and manifested in the workplace are depression and anxiety.

Depression

Even mild depression, called dysthymic disorder, affects a significant number of adults in this country. "Depression is a major public health problem that affects up to 6 million American men and 12 million American women annually."[8]

Table 4.1 explains dysthymic disorder as described in the *Diagnostic and Statistical Manual, Fourth Edition,* (DSM-IV)[9]:

A study that was reported by the American City Business Journals Inc. indicated that "U.S. workers with depressive disorders cost employers $44 billion in lost productive time, compared with $13 billion for those without depression, according to a study by Irving-based AdvancePCS."[10] In an opinion article posted on the same Web site, Barbara Bartlein of Great Lakes Consulting Group writes: "Mental health matters now more than ever. Business success depends on people who are resilient and well-adjusted — motivated employees who can handle complex demands and constant change."[11]

As reported on the Chealth Web site in an article written by Nelly Elayoubi entitled "Depressed Workers Cost Bosses Billions"[12]:

- More than $30 billion is lost in industrial production a year and workers often go untreated.
- About 85 percent of jobs in the United States and Canada require cerebral skills — skills that are impaired by depression or anxiety.

TABLE 4.1   Dysthymic Disorder

- Depressed mood for most of the day, for more days than not, as indicated either by subjective account or observation by others, for at least two years. Note: In children and adolescents, mood can be irritable and duration must be at least one (1) year.
- Presence, while depressed of two (or more) of the following:
  - Appetite decreased or increased
  - Sleep decreased or increased
  - Fatigue or low energy
  - Poor self-image, low self-esteem
  - Reduced concentration or indecisiveness
  - Feels hopeless
- During this two-year period, the above symptoms are never absent longer than two consecutive months.
- During the first two years of this syndrome, the patient has not had a Major Depressive Episode.
- The patient has had no Manic, Hypomanic, or Mixed Episodes.
- The patient has never fulfilled criteria for Cyclothymic Disorder.
- The disorder does not exist solely in the context of a chronic psychosis (such as Schizophrenia or Delusional Disorder).
- The symptoms are not directly caused by a general medical condition or the use of substances, including prescription medications.
- The symptoms cause clinically important distress or impair work, social or personal functioning.

Source: From the Diagnostic and Statistical Manual IV.

Anxiety and Panic Disorders

Anxiety and depression are often "lumped together"; however, an anxiety disorder is very different from depression and is characterized by:

- Psychological symptoms, including:
  - Insomnia
  - Irritability or anger
  - Inability to concentrate
  - Excessive worry and ruminating
  - Free-floating apprehension
  - Feeling unreal and not in control of one's actions (depersonalization)
- A wide range of possible physical symptoms, including some of the following:
  - Abdominal discomfort

- Diarrhea
- Dry mouth
- Rapid heartbeat or palpitations
- Tightness or pain in chest
- Shortness of breath
- Dizziness
- Frequent urination

For more information about depression and anxiety, one can visit the National Institute of Mental Health Web site at http://www.nimh.nih.gov/publicat/depression.cfm.

Post-Traumatic Stress Disorder (PTSD)

Post-Traumatic Stress Disorder (PTSD) is a unique mental disorder that develops directly as a result of exposure to some type of trauma. To qualify for a diagnosis of PTSD, an individual must be exposed to an incident in which he or she feels that his or her life, safety, or emotional integrity has been seriously threatened. Often, for victims who have experienced a traumatic event, they may first be diagnosed with an *adjustment disorder* or an *acute stress disorder*. However, this label is appropriate only for those people whose symptoms remit within 30 days. While many individuals seem to have a built-in resiliency, as many as 20 to 25 percent of victims of trauma remain symptomatic for longer periods of time and therefore may qualify for a diagnosis of PTSD. Vignette 4.1 is an article written by this author for a presentation to the Massachusetts Continuing Legal Education Association. While it includes some (limited) information that is specific to attorneys, it is included here in its entirety as a comprehensive overview of PTSD.

4.1 A Comprehensive Overview of Post-Traumatic Stress Disorder

Introduction

What is now referred to as *Post-Traumatic Stress Disorder* (PTSD) has been around since recorded history under many different designations and descriptions. As recently as the 1800s it was noted that people involved in railroad accidents had emotional distress that was thought to be caused by injury to their spine and were diagnosed with *railroad spine*. Even in the literature, those who have Stephen Crane's *Red Badge of Courage* or *All Quiet On the Western Front* will clearly be able to see all of the signs and symptoms of PTSD as present in these literary accounts of combat from the American Civil War and World War I.

During the U.S. Civil War, *soldier's heart* or *irritable heart* was the name given to a syndrome similar to today's Post-Traumatic Stress Disorder by physician Jacob DaCosta.[1] He later described this syndrome in his paper in 1871 on Irritable Heart. From this, "cardiac neurosis" was the label assigned, as it was thought that the heart was the source of their emotional distress.

Other labels began to emerge through out the 20th century as increasing numbers of soldiers seemed to be suffering from emotional difficulties caused by the experience of combat. *Shell shock* and *combat fatigue* came into vogue during the World Wars along with "combat neurosis" as it became clearer that this was an emotional disorder precipitated by the extreme circumstances of warfare.

Clearly, combat veterans seemed to be the primary group of individuals whose experience resulted in this "new" disorder. However, as the field of psychology developed, it was becoming clearer that even noncombatants were vulnerable to similar symptoms. Janet, one of Freud's earliest colleagues, described, "When people experience *vehement emotions* their minds become incapable of matching their frightening experience with existing cognitive schemes. As a result, memories of the experience cannot be integrated into personal experience and are split off (dissociated)."[2] Freud noted that many of his patients would describe dreams and "flashbacks" in which they were sexually abused or traumatized. Due either to the times or his own personal issues, he determined that these were not real events that had occurred, but rather fantasies that the patient had about adults and coined the theories of Oedipal conflict, penis envy, and castration anxiety, along with the potentially misogynist notion that these accounts of sexual mistreatment were primarily hysterical fantasies of young women.[3] One may argue that had Freud taken these recounted events as reality rather than fantasy, the issues of sexual and physical abuse may have received greater scrutiny many decades before it did.

Later, the labels of *rape trauma syndrome* and *battered child syndrome* were utilized to describe the emotional picture of victims of these tragedies. However, it was not until the 1970–1980s that a clearer understanding of the impact of sexual mistreatment of children developed and it was discerned that the symptomatology of these victims looked very much like those of combat veterans. Thus, PTSD first appeared in the DSM-III as a diagnostic label delineated from other diagnoses and could be applied to a wide variety of individuals who had experienced an intense and traumatic event in their lives. It has now been more than 25 years and the field has grown to have even greater understanding as to how PTSD differs from other diagnoses, the etiology of the disorder, the biological factors and the other types of experiences that may precipitate such a syndrome.

Diagnostic Criteria

PTSD is characterized by a specific group of symptoms that set it apart from other types of psychological disorders. First noted in the DSM-III and now in the DSM-IV, PTSD is described as follows.[4]

Post-Traumatic Stress Disorder (309.81)

- The patient has experienced or witnessed or was confronted with an unusually traumatic event or events that has *both* of these elements:
  - The event(s) involved actual or threatened death or serious physical injury to the patient or to others, *and*
  - The patient felt intense fear, horror or helplessness*
- The patient repeatedly relives the event in at least one of these ways:
  - Intrusive, distressing recollections (thoughts, images)*
  - Repeated, distressing dreams*
  - Through flashbacks, hallucinations or illusions, acts or feels as if the event were recurring (includes experiences that occur when intoxicated or awakening)*
  - Marked mental distress in reaction to internal or external cues that symbolize or resemble the event
  - Physiological reactivity (such as rapid heart beat, elevated blood pressure) in response to these cues
- The patient repeatedly avoids the trauma-related stimuli and has numbing of general responsiveness (absent before the traumatic event) as shown by three or more of:
  - Tries to avoid thoughts, feelings or conversations concerned with the event
  - Tries to avoid activities, people, or places that recall the event
  - Cannot recall an important feature of the event
  - Marked loss of interest or participation in activities important to the patient
  - Feels detached or isolated from other people
  - Restriction in ability to love or feel other strong emotions
  - Feels life will be brief or unfulfilled (lack of marriage, job, children)
- At least two of the following symptoms of hyperarousal were not present before the traumatic event:
  - Insomnia (initial or interval)
  - Irritability
  - Poor concentration
  - Hypervigilance
  - Increased startle response
- The above symptoms have lasted longer than one month.
- These symptoms cause clinically important distress or impair work, social, or personal functioning.

Specify whether:

- *Acute.* Symptoms have lasted less than three months.
- *Chronic.* Symptoms have lasted three months or longer.
- *With Delayed Onset.* The symptoms did not appear until at least six months after the event.

Coding Note

*In children, response to the traumatic event may be agitation or disorganized behavior. Young children may relive the event through repetitive play, trauma-specific reenactment, or nightmares without recognizable content.

The following is a brief(er) summarization of the aforementioned symptoms of PTSD:

The individual had to experience/witness an intense event in their life in which they perceived that they and/or others were in extreme danger.

Re-experiencing symptoms involves a sort of mental replay of the trauma, often accompanied by strong emotional reactions. This can happen in reaction to thoughts or reminders (triggers) of the experience when the person is awake or… in the form of nightmares during sleep. For children the re-experiencing may take the place of reenacting the trauma in play, art, etc.

Avoidance symptoms are often exhibited as efforts to evade activities, places, or people that are reminders of the trauma. The avoidance may be hidden behind a defensive style, or an anxiety disorder/phobic reaction.

Numbing symptoms are typically experienced as a loss of emotions, particularly positive feelings. Alcohol or other drugs may be used to facilitate the numbing.

Arousal symptoms reflect excessive physiological activation and include a heightened sense of being on guard as well as difficulty with sleep and concentration.

The symptoms must persist for over one month, cause significant distress, and affect the individual's ability to function socially, occupationally, or domestically.

"Simple" and "Complex" PTSD

While PTSD is characterized by the aforementioned symptoms, it is understood by mental health professionals that there are two types of PTSD: "simple" and "complex." Complex PTSD (Disorder of Extreme

Stress) is defined as the disorder that results from long-term, ongoing stress, prolonged trauma, especially that is experienced during child-hood or adolescence. Usually it is also characterized by disruptive envi-ronmental conditions and colors the child's total life experience. Examples of this would be ongoing physical or sexual abuse, severe neglect, growing up/living in a war zone, etc. As will be discussed later, it is believed that this type of experience may disrupt the child's normal development, resulting in organic and hormonal changes that can impact memory and emotions (see "The Biology of PTSD"). For adults, the same conditions would apply to the same events as well as being imprisoned, tortured, in combat, etc.

Simple PTSD is the result of one single event that has occurred in the individual's life and is over. Examples range from accidents, assaults, to being the victim of an earthquake, tornado, etc. The event itself has closure and the individual may return to a regular and stable life.

Not all victims of trauma develop PTSD. While many individuals who experience traumatic events may develop PTSD, it is essential to note that not all become symptomatic to the point where they would "qualify" for a diagnosis. Studies after World War II of concentration camp survi-vors indicated that long-term extreme trauma had severe biological, psychological, and social consequences...including a diminished capac-ity to cope with both psychological and biological stressors later in life. However, not all Holocaust survivors had PTSD. In recent years, it seems that the Viet Nam war rocketed the label of PTSD into the regular lexicon of America. Yet, only about 15 percent of Viet Nam veterans suffer(ed) from long-term PTSD.

In a study by Foa and Rothman with victims of rape, 94 percent had symptoms that reached the level of PTSD one week after the assault. After two months, only 52 percent had symptoms at that level and nine months later, only 47 percent of the victims evidenced the diagnostic criterion.

To summarize, "...the experience of traumatic events is extremely common — for example, a random sample of young adults living in urban Detroit found that the prevalence of trauma was 39 percent (Bre-slau et al., 1991). Second, only a percentage of people exposed to a traumatic event go on to develop the picture of PTSD, indicating the importance that vulnerability and resilience factors play in the etiology of the disorder. In the Detroit study, 23.6 percent of those exposed to traumatic events had lifetime PTSD (Breslau et al., 1991). Third, although only some of those exposed develop PTSD, this disorder is nevertheless highly prevalent, with estimated lifetime prevalence of up to 8 or 9 percent in the general population of the United States (Davidson et al., 1991; Helzer et al., 1987; Solomon and Davidson, 1987). In vulnerable communities and high-risk groups, such as war veterans and rape victims, the incidence of PTSD is far higher; 30 percent in war veterans (Kulka et al., 1990), 47 percent of sexual assault victims (Rothbaum et al., 1992)."[5]

It is essential to remember that humans have a great capacity for resiliency and self-healing. To overdiagnose does an injustice to the individuals who truly suffer from PTSD. Further, when working in the legal arena, it is essential to be sure that the plaintiff qualifies for a diagnosis that cannot be refuted by the other side's expert.

The Biology of PTSD

Until recently, the only way to look into the human brain was to wait until the individual died, perform an autopsy, remove the brain, and take gross slices of tissue and look at them under a microscope. This, along with animal studies, allowed for only the most rudimentary observations. With the advent of new technologies such as CAT and PET scans and MRIs, the human brain and its activities may be viewed while the individual remains alive and the brain active. PTSD has always been viewed as primarily a psychological disorder marked by specific symtomatology. Now, studies indicate that there is a significant biological component that may, in fact, be the cause of these psychological symptoms. Although still in the early stages, the findings are pointing to changes in both brain chemistry as well as neuroanatomy. To simplify, the production of neurotransmitters (the chemicals that are produced in the brain and that keep the brain working) seems to be disrupted by acute stress of a significant level and duration. Further, there is evidence to suggest that parts of the brain infrastructure may be underdeveloped as a result of the types of events that result in complex PTSD. Further, these parts of the brain are located in the limbic system, which is thought to be the seat of human emotion. Specifically, the amygdala and the hippocampus are the areas that seem to be uniquely disquieted by trauma. When the brains of victims of PTSD are viewed by the aforementioned technology, it appears as if these areas in the brain are constantly "on" and unable to be regulated as in a normal brain. Thus, intense emotions, hyperarousal, mood swings, and agitation are thought to be the result of this trauma to the brain development or even just the brain chemistry. Further, there is evidence to suggest that parts of the brain may shrink or develop abnormally as a result of traumatic experiences. This may account for the often-seen *co-morbidity* of substance abuse along with the myriad of other manifestations of long-term PTSD. (See "Co-morbidity.")

When working with PTSD victims, I often use the metaphor of a computer that has received a virus and thus experiences significant disruption and corruption of the software. The longer the virus remains on board without "treatment," the greater level of impairment. As individuals attempt to cope with their difficulties, they may develop a wide range of coping mechanisms, including some that are inappropriate or maladaptive, yet these mechanisms provide the ability to put the computer into *sleep mode*, or a *screen freeze*, rather than have a *total system crash*.

The following is a more complex description of some of the recent findings with respect to the biological/neurological issues.

A number of biological factors have been linked to PTSD symptoms. It has been claimed that they make people with PTSD hyper-responsive to stressful stimuli, especially stimuli that are reminiscent of the trauma.

Chronic Stress Reaction

Chronically enhanced secretion of adrenaline and noradrenaline in patients of PTSD are consistent with a chronic stress reaction. In keeping with the enhanced secretion of these stress hormones, patients show enhanced startle response and higher baseline heart rates and blood pressure.

Hypothalamic-Pituitary-Adrenal Axis Abnormalities

Patients with PTSD have abnormally low levels of cortisol. On administration of low-dose dexamethasone, patients exhibit hypersuppression of cortisol, the pattern of findings suggesting enhanced negative feedback in the hypothalamic-pituitary-adrenal axis and that it is set to produce a large response to further stressors.

Neuroendocrinological Abnormalities

Several neurotransmitter systems seem to be dysregulated in PTSD:

- Sensitization of the **noradrenergic system** — in particular, down-regulation of the alpha-2-adrenergic receptors, causing increased levels of noradrenaline and enhanced locus coeruleus activity, explaining in part symptoms of autonomic hyperarousal and re-experiencing (through the effects of beta-adrenergic receptors in the amygdala and cortical structures).
- Sensitization of the **serotonergic system** — serotonin controls the function of septohippocampal behavioral inhibition system, sensitization would lead to activation of the same by mild everyday stressors, explaining in part symptoms of hyperarousal.
- **Endogenous opiates** have been suspected to mediate the symptoms of emotional numbing and amnesia.
- Veterans with PTSD have been found to have enhanced levels of **corticotrophin releasing factor** (CRF) in the cerebrospinal fluid; this might be the reason behind enhanced plasma adrenaline and noradrenaline concentration and the consequent anxiety and fear related behavior.

Thyroid Function

Some studies have detected increased levels of thyroid hormones in PTSD patients, the levels correlating with the severity of hyperarousal symptoms.

Neuroimaging

- Magnetic resonance imaging has shown a reduced **hippocampal volume** in war veterans and women with a history of childhood sexual abuse. Disturbances of hippocampal function may lead to enhanced reactivity to stimulation and deficits in autobiographical memory.
- **Dysfunction of the amygdala** is often considered the key to delay in the extinction of fear responses to reminders of the traumatic event.
- Positron emission tomography has depicted **reduced blood flow in the middle temporal cortex**, which is supposed to play a role in the extinction of fear through inhibition of amygdala function.[6]

A Bio-Psycho-Social Trap:

To sum it up, Shalve and Rogel-Fuchs describe PTSD as a biological-psychological-social trap characterized by (1) a permanent alteration in the *neurobiological* processes that results in hyperarousal; (2) the acquisition of *conditioned* fear/avoidance response to trauma-related stimuli; (3) altered *cognitive* schemata and *social* apprehension that result from the dissonance of the traumatic event and one's previous knowledge of the world.[7]

Other Factors

Much thought has gone into trying to understand why some individuals develop PTSD, while others may develop other or no symptoms after a dramatic incident. A wide range of factors may account for the variance in reactions. While this list is too long to go into detail, it is important to have an understanding of each factor when dealing with victims of PTSD.

- Type and circumstance of incident (e.g., reactions to sexual assault may be very different to those of being a victim of an earthquake)
- Age of the victim at the time of incident
- Duration of the incident
- How much time has elapsed since the incident occurred
- Psychological preparation for the event
- Who/what was the perpetrator/cause of the incident
- Type(s) of injury to the victim
- Multiple or individual victims of the incident
- Prior traumatic incidents in the lives of the individual
- Did the individual keep it a secret or did he receive support
- Other than the traumatic event, does the individual have a stable, supportive lifestyle
- Co-morbidity issues

From both a psychological as well as a legal perspective, these issues may generate a significant orientation to both treatment as well as legal strategy.

The Role of Shame

One of the key features that often accompany a diagnosis of PTSD is shame. So often, there is an underlying sense of responsibility for what has occurred. Or, a faulty perception that perhaps he or she might have been able to avoid the event, perpetrator, accident, etc. Even though they may rationally acknowledge that they were a child at the time or that they had no control over the earthquake or their buddy died as a result of a firefight with the enemy, or the rapist assaulted them in their hotel room, there is often an underlying sense of culpability. This sense of guilt and shame is what often leads to greater levels of depression, and suicidality… especially if others in their familial or social circle mirror any of this dynamic. Further, these potential improbabilities are often played upon by the defending side of legal cases. The questioning of plaintiffs around these issues may generate a significant amount of distress, leading to an intensification of psychological impairment. The client must understand and be well prepared for this type of "retraumatization."

As Terrance Real describes in his book, *I Don't Want to Talk about It,* when dealing with trauma there are two levels: *active* trauma and *passive* trauma.[8] Active trauma is the actual event or incident that has resulted in the injury. Passive trauma refers to the response of others… or lack thereof. As an example, consider a victim of sexual assault, certainly a dramatic and traumatic event. This would be considered the active trauma. Let us further consider the further emotional impact upon her if her husband or parents responded with the non-nurturing attitude of blaming her for being "in the wrong place" or wearing seductive clothing. Another example might be the woman who has the active trauma of a surgery that disfigures her body and the passive trauma of her husband rejecting her sexually. Even on a national level, one can see the interaction between active and passive trauma when one reviews how 18- to 20-year-old Viet Nam era soldiers were sent into combat for a year and then were rejected upon their return to the United States, often labeled as "baby killers," "war criminals," etc. What we understand about trauma is that many people have a natural inborn resiliency that can help them manage and move beyond many terrible and awful situations and events. However, what is most devastating is not the active, but rather the passive trauma as it plays on the guilt and shame that must be resolved as part of the recovery process.

Co-morbidity

The lifestyles of victims of unresolved (and often untreated) PTSD are often characterized by a range of other problems and difficulties. With mood, hyperarousal, and avoidance being difficult to regulate, the individual may be vulnerable to self-medicating with drugs or alcohol. In addition, relationships may be fraught with intense bouts of overreactive anger accompanied by distance and remoteness. This, in combination with guilt and shame, may result in a lifestyle punctuated by impulsivity, poor judgment, risk-taking behaviors, substance abuse, and further incidents of victimization. Clinicians often see patients whose "computer" has been severely infected by a virus to the point where it has interfered with many of individual's "programs." Getting to the core PTSD issues often means dealing with a wide variety of other "surface" issues such as drug/alcohol, relational, and occupational issues. Many victims of complex PTSD may not present as the most appropriate of clients.

PTSD in the Workplace

With increasing frequency, more cases are coming forward where the workplace or individuals within are seen as the perpetrators or cause of extreme of stress. Sexual harassment, bullying, wrongful termination, intimidating management style, assault, and witness of violence have been cited as the cause of severe emotional duress. While perhaps not rising to the level of PTSD, a number of these types of cases have been settled against the work organization. While this paper cannot cover this topic in appropriate detail, one may review some of the recent cases by visiting the Web site www.bullyonline.org/stress/ptsd.htm#Legal.

References

1. T. Lewis, *The Soldier's Heart and the Effort Syndrome,* Paul B. Hoeber, New York, 1919.
2. B.A. van der Kolk and L. McFarlane, Editors, *Traumatic Stress,* Guildord Press, New York, 1996, p. 52.
3. B.A. van der Kolk and L. McFarlane, Editors, *Traumatic Stress,* Guildord Press, New York, 1996, p. 52.
4. American Psychiatric Association, *Diagnostic and Statistical Manual of Mental Disorders,* American Psychiatric Association, Washington, D.C., 2000.
5. www.brainexplorer.org/ptsd/PTSD.
6. www.twilightbridge.com/psychiatryproper/ailmentguide/ptsd/bio.htm.
7. A.Y. Shalev, Y. Rogel-Fuchs, and R.K. Pitman, Conditioned Fear and Psychological Trauma (Editorial), *Biological Psychiatry,* 31, 863–856, 1992.
8. T. Real, *I Don't Want to Talk about It,* Scribner Book Company, 1997.

"PTSD for Dummies"

One of the metaphors that this author uses when teaching about or working with victims of PTSD is that of a computer. When an individual experiences trauma, it is as if the brain has an overload of too much information all at once and cannot process it. The sensory input is intense and coming in from all modalities: visual, auditory, olfactory, and tactile (touch). It is analogous to a computer that is running too many programs at the same time and trying to process or download too much information. Many of us may have had the experience of the computer becoming overwhelmed and experiencing a shutdown, as evidenced by a "screen freeze." No matter how much you bang on the machine, it will not budge from the last image that was on the screen just before it crashed. It is as if the computer is experiencing a flashback of the trauma. The only thing that can be done is to reboot the computer and hope that you had saved your data. Unfortunately, it is not as simple to reboot the human brain. However, there are interventions and treatments that actually are analogous to rebooting and reprogramming a computer. Another way of explaining what happens to humans who experience a significant event that may result in PTSD is to once again use the computer metaphor. The trauma acts as a virus that affects the software of the computer. Anyone who has had the experience of a virus in his or her computer will understand that it is an insidious influence that can wreak havoc with the proficiency of one's computer. In much the same way, trauma can get into the brain and severely impact one's social, emotional, and even cognitive programming.

One of the other things that is understood about victims of trauma and severe crisis is that it is not a cognitive experience. What is meant is that although the individual may know that the event is over cognitively, the inner brain, which houses the emotional center, does not pay attention to what the cognitive center has to say about an event. The emotional center does not have a sense of time or place. It may be easily triggered by any stimulus that may be associated with it. One of the most dramatic examples of this was when this author was working with a Viet Nam veteran who had spent much time in combat. One day about 20+ years after leaving Viet Nam, he was cutting his lawn. It had been raining for quite a number of weekends, and he had not been able to get to it on a regular basis and now the grass was too tall for his mower. Therefore, he had to cut it by hand with a machete. He reported that the action of cutting the grass with the machete, along with the smell of the cut grass and the heat and humidity, resulted in a flashback to a similar action in Viet Nam when he had to cut through the jungle. Although he cognitively knew that he was not there, the emotional center of his brain had been activated by the sensory stimuli and reproduced images and emotions of the original trauma.

Another dramatic workplace event was one in which there had been an explosion at a factory that killed three workers and seriously injured three others. One of the injured workers spent a month in the hospital recovering from burns. Upon release, he looked forward to returning to work and assuming his usual responsibilities. However, almost immediately upon entering the building and going to his workstation near where the explosion took place, he experienced an overwhelming panic attack and ran from the building. Unfortunately, he never was able to return to work in that facility. In fact, he gave up riding motorcycles and could only light his cigarettes with regular matches… not lighters. Both the motorcycles and lighters activated an intense fear of gas explosion. It should also be noted that this individual was not a wimp by any stretch of the imagination. He had been in numerous fights, motorcycle accidents, and even spent time in jail. Part of what was so emotionally disruptive and shaming for him was the acknowledgment that he was now afraid… a new emotion for him.

This point is being made (and perhaps over-made) at some length because it is important to understand that people who experience traumatic events can experience a recurrence or escalation of the event for some time afterward. Further, it must be understood that it is usually not a case of malingering or emotional weakness if one has this type of reaction. Finally, the entire brain gets overloaded, and the cognitive center that helps us process emotional experiences can be rendered impotent. When working with victims, current best practices suggest that interventions that involve both a cognitive (left brain) as well as an emotional/esthetic (right brain) component seem to provide the best results. Therefore, a combination of modalities such as talk therapy, medication, support groups, exercise, art, massage, and yoga could be used in combination as a viable prescription.

Similarly, to truly understand PTSD, it is not enough just to use the cognitive center of one's brain (by reading this material), but to involve the total brain to conceptualize the experience.

Substance Abuse

As described in the preceding material, while the stigma surrounding mental health issues has lessened, it still remains and individuals suffering may not seek out services. Further, many people do not recognize that they are experiencing a clinical problem, but rather just see it as a part of life or "just the way things are." Many wind up self-managing or self-medicating their condition with a variety of remedies. For many, using other substances such as alcohol, drugs, "process addictions" (gambling, sex, porn, Internet, shopping, etc.), and abuse of medication becomes a bigger problem than the original condition. As discussed previously, the co-morbidity of substance abuse is often seen as the primary problem, and it is not until the individual begins to deal with that that they might discover the underlying mood disorder, childhood abuse or trauma, or current lifestyle issues that have impacted their psychology and the connection between the maladaptive efforts to manage the symptoms and their over-involvement with substances. Even now, in many cultures, it is more acceptable for people to acknowledge, "Well, I have a drinking problem," than "Well, I have a mental/emotional problem."

Family Reactions

Health issues of any type are a family condition. Whether it be a physical problem or an emotional one, the effect on family members may be equally if not, at times, more dramatic than on the individual who is the patient. There are many occasions when the individual who experiences a traumatic event seems to come through it with minimal reactions. Yet, someone in their family may have a more pronounced reaction. As an example, there may be a flood that effects an entire area. While certain workers may want to return to duty as soon as possible, they may find that their family members are having a difficult time. The individual may experience role conflict... to whom do they owe allegiance... family or work?

Two films do a compelling job of portraying reactions to trauma. It is recommended that the reader view these two movies — *Door in the Floor* and *Fearless* — to see how trauma impacted these individuals and their families and the role that re-experiencing, depression, shame, and co-morbidity plays in these dramas.

Critical Incident Stress

This author wrote his first book, *Critical Incident Stress and Trauma in the Workplace* (1994), which described the advancing concept of *critical incident stress (CIS)*. Developing from the work of Jeffrey Mitchell, who first wrote about CIS, the book describes the impact of workplace trauma on rescue personnel, as well as the victims themselves. What is now known in the field is that both the victim, as well as the caregiver, can develop significant reactions to a traumatic event. While not considered a clinical diagnosis, CIS can be experienced by public safety and emergency service professionals. In recent years, articles have appeared describing the numbers of police, fire, and rescue workers and utility workers who worked at Ground Zero. Three years later, many are still suffering from emotional reactions as a result of their work at Ground Zero. Often, these reactions appear similar to those of PTSD; and for many who work in the crisis care professions, there is a vulnerability to developing an emotional condition that could meet the diagnostic criteria of PTSD. The concept of critical incident stress is discussed briefly in a later chapter of this book. However, for a more detailed understanding of this concept, please read the aforementioned book by this author.

References

1. H. Seyle, *The Stress of Life*, McGraw-Hill, New York, 1978.
2. H. Benson, *The Relaxation Response*, William Morrow & Co., New York, 1975.
3. J. Ivancevich and M. Matteson, *Organizational Behavior Management*, McGraw-Hill, New York, 2002, p. 266.
4. T.H. Holmes and R.H. Raye, The Social Readjustment Rating Scale, *Journal of Psychosomatic Research*, 11, 213–218, 1967.
5. Sick of Work: Always on the Job, Employees Pay with Health, by John Schwartz, *New York Times*, September 13, 2004.
6. J. Ivancevich and M. Matteson, *Organizational Behavior Management*, McGraw-Hill, New York, 2002, p. 280.
7. www.nmha.org/may/fastfacts.cfm.
8. www.nmha.org/may/fastfacts.cfm.
9. The American Psychiatric Association, *The Diagnostic and Statistical Manual of Mental Disorders (DSM-IV)*, The American Psychiatric Association, Washington, D.C., 2000.
10. Taken from www.bizjournals.com.
11. Taken from www.bizjournals.com.
12. Taken from chealth.canoe.ca/health_news_detail.asp?channel_id=11&news_id=10609.

Chapter 5

The Lifespan of a Crisis, Trauma, Disaster, Catastrophe

Take a moment to think about a personal crisis or event that you (the reader) have experienced during your adult life. It should be something that was of significant impact — perhaps the sudden death of a loved one, a serious surgical procedure, getting married, having a child, getting divorced, having to relocate to a new home in another state, being laid off from a job. These are samples of "normal" life events that many of us might experience. As this chapter describes the stages and phases, you should consider your specific event in an effort to see if the stages "fit" with your own personal experience.

Often, it is not understood that significant events have a life cycle that might continue on long after the initial incident has concluded. Be it a death of a loved one, a surgical procedure, a divorce, a layoff, floods, 9/11, or warfare, the participants (victims) go through stages and phases of recovery. In the 1970s, Dr. Elizabeth Kubler-Ross wrote her initial book, *On Death and Dying*,[1] in which she proposed that when people receive a diagnosis of a life-threatening illness, they go through psychological stages: shock, denial, bargaining, anger, depression, and acceptance. This author can remember having meetings with other professionals, discussing whether a person was in the bargaining stage or the denial stage. Were they depressed or angry? Having attended numerous workshops with Dr.

Kubler-Ross, she made it clear that it was not a rigid set of stages through which the individuals go, but rather that these are phases or emotional transitions that can all be experienced at different times and in different sequences... sometimes all together.

Others have also developed a stage/phase paradigm through which individuals move as they attempt to cope with trauma and tragedy. While neither intending nor attempting to *reinvent the wheel*, this author divides the process into five different phases. Further, not all people who have experienced an event have the same reactions or proceed at the same rate through these phases or stages. However, it is important to understand that these are not rigid parameters, but rather characteristics or features that can be experienced during a certain sequence in the process. **Further, the same may hold true for a group of people, whether they be a family, a community, or a work organization.** In addition, it should be noted that each one of these stages coincides with Maslow's hierarchy of needs (see Table 1.1 in Chapter 1).

Survival Phase (0 to 72 hours)

During this time of acute reaction, the individual might be in an extreme state of emotional (and/or physical) distress. As an example, during a surgical procedure, the individual would be in surgery, then in recovery, receiving medications, and with limited capacity to take care of his or her biological needs. Or, if an individual receives word of the sudden and unexpected death of a loved one, the emotional impact of such news may render him or her unable to process information and proceed with many activities of daily living. Or, as in the case with a large-scale catastrophe such as an earthquake or 9/11, people are just trying to survive, connect with family, and may be in a state of "shell shock." Even the community and the rescue efforts can go through a stage of disorganization before a coordinated plan of action is brought to bear. This phase may last (roughly) from 1 to 3 days after an incident. People usually require basic needs such as food, shelter, relief from pain, and connection with family and near friends. They may be in a state of physical or emotional shock and not able to process the incident or its impact. It is a time for quiet consolation, a compassionate presence, and caring for basic biological needs. Going back to the example of the death of a loved one, it is a time when the individual may need to be surrounded by close friends and family and cared for with food and emotional support. This is where crisis care professions (police, fire, hospital, clergy, etc.) are instrumental in the initial management of a situation. This survival stage coincides with Maslow's first stage: physiological.

Support

It is at this time that the individual or group begins to get an accurate assessment of the nature and impact of the incident. The state of shock gradually diminishes and the reality sets in. This phase transitions from the former and can last up to the next one to two weeks, depending upon the circumstances and nature of the event. In the case of the death of a loved one, funeral plans are made, family is coming together, and depending upon religious orientation, formal condolences are implemented. Or, in the case of a large-scale incident, rescue and recovery operations are in full swing, shelters have been set up, and emergency management departments have developed a formalized operational strategy. Or, in the case of a patient who has been hospitalized, he or she is now transferred from recovery or the ICU to a regular medical floor, rehabilitation center, or even home. This is the phase in which professional services (funeral directors, emergency management personnel, social service agencies, clergy, temporary shelters, etc.) are brought to bear. In addition, the familial and personal social support networks become very involved. Once again, note that this phase coincides with Maslow's second level of need satisfaction: safety and security.

Adjustment

We are now about one to four months out from the original incident. This next phase is often the most difficult. It is the time when the individual must start to transition back to a "normal" life. Be it a death of a loved one, surgery, or even a dramatic catastrophe, there comes a time when the expectation is that "life must go on." Kids go back to school, people must return to work, shelters begin to close as people go back to their damaged homes, the patient leaves the hospital, etc. This phase is usually an extended period as the individual faces the realities of the situation. Unfortunately, it is often a time when support drops away. For example,

- Funerals are over and the condolence visits and notes stop coming.
- Stitches have already been removed and physical therapy has begun.
- The layoff has taken effect and unemployment is in place, and the arduous task of looking for a new job has begun.
- The floods have receded and now it is time to pick through the rubble and deal with insurance agencies and other bureaucracies.
- The workplace is indicating that it is time to return to your usual and expected duties and responsibilities.

- Children need a parent, oftentimes now more than ever.
- The expectations are that financial, social, and occupational responsibilities must be assumed in full measure.

For most, it is a very difficult time when the expectations are demanding a return to usual and customary duties and responsibilities. It is often a period when people begin to falter and to evidence signs of emotional or social distress. Take as examples these two scenarios:

A woman is diagnosed with breast cancer and has a mastectomy. After three days, she is discharged home with visiting nurse care. After six weeks of home care, it is determined that she can return to work. Initially, her return is met with much attention and emotional fanfare, with cards and flowers on her desk. However, by the second week back, the flowers have wilted along with the emotional support, and she is beginning to find that it is difficult for her to keep up with her workload. In addition, she has had to go for follow-up visits to her surgeon and is beginning to "think about" reconstruction surgery and may need to be out of work again for two weeks. Co-workers who were "covering" for her during her absence now expect to have some relief because she is back to work. However, they find that "she is not her old self," is making mistakes, and is unable to produce as she did prior to her absence.

A bank was robbed by armed perpetrators who were shouting loudly with threats and swearing, and even fired their weapons into the ceiling of the bank. The employees and customers were herded into an area of the lobby and told to lie on the floor with their faces down and eyes closed. One customer was shoved down roughly and hurt his arm and knee. The robbers then completed the robbery and left the bank. After the alarm was sounded and police and bank security responded, the employees were interviewed and finally allowed to go home about four hours later. It was determined by bank administration to give the employees two days off. All reported back to work, with the bank's expectation that it was all over, no one was truly hurt, and "let's get back to business as usual." For the first week, all went well for most of the employees because there was a lot of support from administration as well as customers, along with increased police surveillance. Within a week or so, one employee began to experience problems with nightmares, difficulty falling asleep, or early morning awakening. Another employee began to have anxiety symptoms, leading to panic feelings when she was driving to work. The first employee began to call in sick and the other came to work but his concentration was impaired, took frequent breaks, and made several significant errors. As these problems were causing job performance difficulties, both were being counseled by the branch manager by the second or third week. In response, the employee with the sleep problem went to her physician, who "wrote her out" for a six-week short-term disability. The other employee sought services from the bank's employee assistance program (EAP). In both cases, it was determined that the difficulties and the job performance impairment resulted from the bank robbery incident. Morale within the branch began to falter as some thought that the employee was a malingerer while others thought that the bank was being insensitive. Request for transfers to other branches began to be submitted.

Both of these cases demonstrate that it is often not until the *adjustment* phase that individuals or organizations begin to bump into the reality of the incident. This phase can last up to the first year after an incident as seasons, holidays, birthdays, and anniversaries are celebrated. Or, as scars form and the reality of disfigurement or disability are coped with; or as homes are repaired, rebuilt, or relocated; or as job interviews are conducted, offers are awaited, and hopes are raised and lowered. Once again, this coincides with level three of Maslow's needs: belonging, social, and love.

Resolution

Resolution lasts approximately 6–18 months. It is the phase when people begin to accommodate to their new life. They are no longer bumping into the day-in and day-out harsh realities of the trauma, crisis, or transition. They have begun to establish new coping strategies, resources, and supports. No longer does the event seem to be the primary focus of their day. However, there are still issues and incidents that must be dealt with that are the residual from the original incident. This stage coincides with Maslow's fourth level: self-esteem.

Re(dis)covery

Re(dis)covery lasts 2+ years. It is the term that this author uses rather than *recovery*. Recovery is synonymous with healing, mending, and (incorrectly) a misconception that there will be a return to the original state-of-being established prior to the incident. As described in a previous chapter, one can consider this the *premorbid* state. Unfortunately, for most people who experience significant crises or tragedies in their lives, this is usually not possible after a significant event. If one thinks of an individual recovering from an event such as a divorce or death, or an organization recovering from a layoff or a reorganization, or a community that has experienced a flood or an earthquake, these types of incidents are "life changers," be it for the individual, family, community, or work organization. As much as it may be desired, things do not "return to normal." Rather, there is a painful ordeal when the system struggles to resolve and recover. Part of what makes the recovery process difficult and painful is the acknowledgment that things are different. Things will never be the same. The acceptance of this is often a crucial step in the healing process, be it an individual, a family, or a work organization. This reminds this author of a time when he was working with a patient who had been one of the victims of a factory explosion in which three were killed and several (including himself) were seriously injured. After several months of therapy, he asked, "When am I going to be my old self?" Although the exact reply is not remembered, it was gently communicated to him that, as disruptive as it may be to hear this, in all likelihood he will not return to his old self, and that this should not be the goal… trauma is a life changer… and he will mend and rediscover a new self. Hopefully, a stronger self as a result of what he has gone through. What we are really talking about is the formation of a new self-concept or self-identity that incorporates the incident into the fabric of the individual's life… the family's life, the corporation's life, or as in the case with 9/11, the nation's life. Crisis and trauma forge new cultural shifts, new dynamics, and new experiences. As a personal example, this author went through a divorce about ten years ago. For a period of time, it seemed that he was bumping into his original life, having difficulty sorting out things: What to do at the holidays? How to be with my children? Who were my friends, and who were those of my ex-wife? Where was I going to live? How do I tell my colleagues that the psychologist was unable to keep his own marriage together? I can remember going to a high school reunion and feeling the embarrassment when asked how was my wife? It took upwards of two years for my new identity to form as a divorced man. To no longer feel the sense of shame; to establish a new and different relationship with my children; to be able return to providing couples therapy; to be able to use the experience professionally… as being written about here. (That is not to say that this author has reached self-actualization, but this phase does coincide with Maslow's fifth level of need satisfaction.)

Groups of People Can Go through Stages and Phases

Groups also go through the phases and stages. Take, for example, a layoff in an organization. The first stage is survival; people find out who is going to survive the layoff and who is not. After that, there might be a brief support phase during which some efforts are made to help the employees. Oftentimes, this is not the case and, as David Noer in his book, *Healing the Wounds,*[2] describes, the survivor victims are often like a combat troop that has survived a military encounter and suffered casualties. While the individuals who were laid off certainly experience a significant crisis, they may have outplacement services and unemployment, and have moved on to the new endeavor of trying to find new employment. Often, the attitude (from management) toward those still employed is that "You should be happy just to have your job." As Noer explains, survivor victims of layoffs often have a mini-version of PTSD with survivor guilt and anger at the management and the lack of support. Further, there is the spoken or often-unspoken expectation that the organization is going to "return to business as usual." Adjustment or reactions on the part of the remaining workers is not acknowledged, expected, or managed. Yet, as is the case with the aforementioned events, these types of crises proceed through similar stages and it is around two to six months later that departments begin to experience decreases in morale, inter- or intra-department conflicts, decreases in productivity, etc.

In much the same way, it should not be expected that a work organization will recover in the sense of returning to its original parameters, cultural dynamics, and organizational paradigms. Instead, after a certain amount of time and the resolving of new boundaries, relationships, inter- and intra-departmental communications and conflicts, etc., the organization rumbles and grumbles to form a new identity. Some personnel stay, while others move on. In talking to people who survive these transitions, they often describe it as a tumultuous time that is fraught with much stress, disorganization, in-fighting, and a sense of uncertainty. The culture has been dismantled or at least diminished. It no longer provides the same sense of stability and consistency. It is usually a time of turmoil before a new organization is in place.

If organizations do make an effort to respond to the human factor, it is usually a very time-limited and half-hearted endeavor, with minimal provision of HR or EAP services metered out during the first week after an organizational transition. Unfortunately, it is often a "too little, too soon" situation that provides little benefit to the individuals or the organization.

Chapter 6

The Five "Rs"

Remain at home, **Retain** at work, **Release** to go home or shelter, **Relocate/reassign** to another facility, **Return** to a previous facility

Different situations require different plans for all or part of the workforce. Where do they go, what do we do with them? Who do we need?

Whenever a workplace must make a decision to **retain** workers (shelter in place), **release** workers, or tell them not to come into work (**remain** at home), it usually connotes a significant disruption fraught with operational, financial, reputational, as well as emotional impact. Depending on the length of time away, **relocating/reassigning** people to temporary placements and then **returning** them to their original work facility may be fraught with stress. This chapter looks at incidents in which these types of management decisions are made and the impact that is generated on the workforce.

Contingency 1: Short-Term Release and Return

This might be an incident in which the employees are temporarily released from work but remain on site. Examples include bomb scares, fire drills, and other incidents that require evacuation of the premises. While most people have experienced such incidents with a limited amount of stress, since 9/11 there has been a heightened level of apprehension concerning even a simple fire drill.

Comprehensive Evacuation Plan

While it is assumed that most work organizations have evacuation plans, I have been surprised by the number of workplaces that do not have such plans in place. Further, some of them are very "skimpy" in terms of their organization and implementation. While every aspect cannot be determined for each type of organization, the following will illustrate some of the points that should be taken into account.

What is recommended for most organizations includes:

- Evacuation plans with predetermined exit paths. These should be posted in a variety of places. In fact, employees should have copies posted in their workspaces and easily visible to them and visitors.
- A predetermined meeting area outside the building. Large organizations should have specific areas for each department, etc.
- Each department or area should have specific people who are designated as "counters" who keep track to make sure that all are accounted for. Receptionists or security responsible for signing in guests and issuing visitor passes should take the list with them to be sure that visitors are also accounted for.
- There should be other people who are "first aiders" who receive some basic first-aid training and have a small "go kit" supplied with water, eye baths, bandages, flashlights, etc.
- Each department should determine those individuals who may need assistance in exiting the building and assign members to facilitate their leaving the building.
- People should have mini-lights on their key chains or chemical "snap lights" in case of a power outage.
- Unless there is an urgent and immediate need for evacuation, people should be instructed to gather their personal belongings such as coats, keys, etc., before exiting the facility. (This author knows that this one might meet with some resistance from security, but to take 30 seconds to return to one's workstation may not be critical.)
- If emergency equipment has been distributed, it should be kept in a specific location and be immediately available.
- Practice the evacuation several times during the year.

Contingency 2: Release and Short-Term Relocation (e.g., power outage, weather, etc.)

This is similar to Contingency 1; however, in this situation, people are told to go home, to another location, or to a shelter. In this case, workers will need to know how to get information regarding when (or where) to return to work. In addition to the evacuation plans of Contingency 1, it is recommended that there be an "800" number that people can call to hear the latest updated information. Further, it is critical to have an up-to-date phone/e-mail list of all employees. While understanding the concern for personal privacy, this list should include home phone numbers, cell phone numbers, and e-mail addresses.

The Need for Instant Communication

Until recently, the method of getting information out to workers was rather hit-or-miss and haphazard. There would be a hierarchical phone chain from administrative level to department heads, to managers, to workers; each individual in the chain knowing whom he or she should be calling. (Public schools are familiar with this as they often have done a similar phone chain to notify about snow days, etc.) In recent years, many organizations have become aware of and utilize a more technologically advanced service where one individual can make a single phone message that goes out to all employees. This might be considered a "pricey" service for some organizations; however, it is certainly a more efficient method of providing information to all in real-time.

In both Contingency 1 and 2 (if possible), it is very helpful to have the senior staff on the street circulating among the employees either during the evacuation or as people are being released. The visibility of senior management at times of stress can serve as a calming influence. When one thinks of 9/11, it is exactly what New York Mayor Rudy Guiliani did during the first days. He floated among the people, trying to provide some degree of comfort and reassurance.

Contingency 3: Short-Term Relocation or Reassignment to Alternative Work Site (e.g., fire, flood, etc.)

If people are moving to an already operating workspace and might be displacing other workers, this could result in a significant disruption. This was the situation for many of the financial organizations after 9/11. People from New York City offices were relocated to New Jersey, upper state New York, and Connecticut offices. In some cases, people had to double up on office space or cubicles, etc. In addition to issues of commuting, there were also problems with displacing other workers from their workspace.

Further, people would now be commuting to a new location, working with people they do not know. If it is known that the situation will resolve in a short period of time, then the people may remain somewhat isolated and disconnected from the regular workers at that site.

As discussed in a previous chapter, if there has been a large-scale catastrophe such as a flood or earthquake in which the employees' homes have been affected, then there is the issue of dealing with distance from family members and social network. This too can be a stressful situation for the workers whose space is being intruded upon.

Contingency 4: Long-Term Reassignment or Non-Return (e.g., major incident, facility closing, etc.)

This was the situation in 2001, when the U.S. Postal Service discovered that the building in Washington, D.C., was infected with Anthrax and two people died. People were reassigned to several other work locations for two years while the investigation was taking place and the building was totally rehabbed and disinfected. Two years is a long time; people had established work relationships. Some were apprehensive about returning despite the medical and technical evidence that the building was now clean. Some wished not to return for a number of other reasons, while others were ready to go back with little issue.

When the time came to return people back to the building, I was involved as a consultant working with a team of people to do the best job possible with this transition. I had wanted to use the U.S. Postal Service's efforts as a "case study" of how an organization tries to do the right thing when faced with an overwhelming task. However, it was requested that I not to go into any specific detail. I will put forth some of the suggestions that I came up with as the outside consultant to their team. I will also say that I believe that they devoted a significant amount of time, effort, resources, and money to making the transition as palatable as possible.

The following are some of the salient features of the consultation that I provided to the U.S. Postal Service. The team worked very hard to implement these and others components.

- Bring personnel back to the site, from the top down (i.e., upper management first, then supervisory, then nonsupervisory). This is discussed in greater detail in Chapter 9.
- All-day supervisor training with 30 attendees in each grouping to deal with their concerns and issues and train them on how to deal with their employees. Ideally, this is to be done at the facility. The second-best option is to have it done elsewhere. Ideally, have the training done within seven to ten days of the plant opening.
- Upper management should be present at each training to give a brief "pep talk."

- The day-long program should be interactive, and not a "talking head" production. There should be small group discussions with an emphasis on how to deal with the questions and concerns that they may have.
- Develop a FAQ sheet that can be distributed to all employees and addresses some of the common concerns.
- "Virtual tours" using videos and still pictures of the rehabbed facility should be made available to all employees at their present site(s).
- Establish a call-in number where employees can leave a message and have their specific question or concern addressed in a timely manner (within one or two days).
- Nonsupervisory personnel should be reoriented in groups and receive a tour from their supervisor. Ideally, this should be done the day before the actual work is to begin. Each supervisor should go through a one- to two-hour orientation meeting with his or her staff. Workers are then dismissed with the expectation that they will return the next day for regular work assignments.
- At the end of the shift on the first day, supervisors should end 15 minutes early to "check in" with group.
- There should be high visibility of senior management on orientation day and first work week.
- EAP and medical staff should also be visible to employees.

Contingency 5: Retaining at Work

There are three situations when employees might be retained at work. One is for their own safety (sheltered in place); the second might be when there is a criminal investigation and law enforcement institutes this order (see Chapter 7, "Legal and Litigation Aspects of Crises, Traumas, and Workplace Disruptions"); and the third is when employees are needed to provide critical services at times of catastrophes. There are a few occasions when workers will be *sheltered at work* rather than be evacuated. These might occur if there is an armed perpetrator in or outside the building, or if there has been a sudden calamitous event in the local area. Or, perhaps some other type of incident has occurred that has created a potentially hazardous environment. At the October 2004 New England Disaster Response Information Exchange (NEDRIX) conference, I participated as one of the experts at the final simulation on the last day of the conference. The scenario was one in which a financial institution had a fake Anthrax scare as part of a larger scenario. While many participating in the simulation felt that the best strategy would be to immediately evacuate the facility, the HAZMAT expert who sat on the panel with myself and a security expert indicated that any contamination had already taken place and that the immediate response should be to shut down the HVAC and to retain workers in the facility. Each person could then be immediately tested to determine if they were contaminated. He further pointed out that while it is not so easy to become contaminated with Anthrax as people may suspect, were people to leave, they might inadvertently take the Anthrax with them and contaminate others outside the building.

While there are other situations that might require retaining employees at work, it is usually done to provide shelter and safety and to deal with security issues. While retaining people at work may be a part of a plan, it should be noted that one cannot force people to stay within a facility. In fact, only law enforcement personnel and some healthcare professionals have the power to contain and restrain people under specific orders. Therefore, it is strongly recommended that any retaining policies or sheltering-in-place interventions should be determined ahead of time and be made clear to all personnel when they can be exercised. One of the major learning points from the NEDRIX simulation exercise was the need for training and education of personnel around this issue.

Finally, certain professions are expected to remain on duty to provide 24/7 operations, especially at times of crisis. These might include healthcare, law enforcement, and utilities as the obvious. However, one must remember hotel personnel, local roads and highway personnel, university or college personnel, etc. If certain staff members are considered critical or essential, then this must be decided beforehand, and each member of this cadre of staff should be prepared for this possibility. It must also be understood that this situation places the individuals in situations of great stress, as it not only affects them, but their families as well if there is a major catastrophe that has affected the local region. In Chapter 7, there is a hospital situation in which hospital personnel were disciplined (and some terminated) for not reporting to duty as scheduled. This type of situation must be avoided at all costs as the ripple effect causes a great deal of toxicity.

The following is recommended:

- In addition to any policies or protocols where this might be stated, it is essential to meet periodically with this group to delineate the roles and expectations.
- Have a biannual drill.
- It should be required that each individual develop a Family Crisis Plan that would include the following:
  - Determine who should be notified (and how) if the employee must remain on duty.

- Determine the *personal* responsibilities that may not be done if this person must remain at work (e.g., daycare pick-up, dog walking, carpool, other part-time job, aged parent who needs some assistance).
- Each family should develop an action plan regarding how it will operate to cover the aforementioned duties.
- Determine how different family members will communicate with each other.

■ Some work organizations suggest that the individuals on this team keep a spare change of clothes, hygiene apparel, medication, etc., in the workplace or the trunks of their cars, should the need arise for them to stay in place.

■ If these people are activated and must stay on duty, there should be a policy whereby they receive some time off as well as some debriefing services (discussed in Chapter 9).

■ Unless specific training precludes others, this team should be rotated to include all staff members.

■ Arrangements should be made to shelter immediate family members of "critical" staff.

It should be noted that there may be a variety or combination of the aforementioned contingencies. Regardless, employees need to have training programs and orientation programs that describe these situations and the expectations of the workplace should they be implemented. Employees may need a time to express concerns, ask questions, and receive information. This is far better than having to implement these directives at the time of a real crisis.

Real-Life Learning

In early 2002, this author provided consultation to one of the financial institutions located a block from Ground Zero with a view of the "pit" from its office windows. While some technical personnel reentered the building that same day, the majority relocated to other facilities in New Jersey, Connecticut, and New York. About a month later, plans were made to have workers transition back to the main buildings. Workers would have to return while it was still a crime scene, surrounded by police, the military, and a wide range of security. They would look out their windows to observe bodies being recovered. The pit was still smoldering and the air quality was questionable. Initially, the idea was to "have people just get on with it and return to work." However, after some discussion, it was clear that there should have been a transition plan because the people were still deeply affected by the event.

This author worked closely with Dr. Leo Flanagan, the head of leadership development for this company. Flanagan was instrumental in implementing programs and policies to facilitate the reentry and reorientation of personnel back into the building. We have spoken on several occasions since then and with more than two years retrospective, he points out several key concepts that were put in place to mitigate the potential impact:

- *Orientation meetings that took place while the employees were still in their relocation placements.* While employees were still deployed to other locations, there were group debriefings to discuss the return to the main building. Subject matter experts were available to answer a wide range of questions such as security, health hazards, work issues, etc.

- *Group tours of the building prior to reentry to work.* People were taken in groups from their temporary work sites, via ferries and buses, through security into the building for a brief tour. No one worked that day. Instead, they toured the building and then returned home as a group.

- *Availability of upper management.* Management was highly visible on the first days of reentry in the lobby of the building to greet the employees as they went through the phalanx of law enforcement and security personnel.

- Availability of EAP, HR, and Occupational Health Services. These services were highly visible, "floating" through the offices rather than waiting for people to come to them.

- *Dissemination of medical information.* There was a wide range of medical information made available to all employees regarding health issues.

- *The little things were often the big issues:* "How do I get to work now?" "Where do we eat since the courtyard has been destroyed?" "I don't want to look out my window at the hole." "My child is scared about me working here and has nightmares."

- *Do not send an out-of-town administrative person to manage the crisis.* The attitude can be that "You are not one of us and you were not there."

- *Ongoing support.* Such support is required for a long time.

- *Information is critical.* This will be discussed in Chapter 9.

Chapter 7

Legal and Litigation Aspects of Crises, Traumas, and Workplace Disruptions

While weapons of mass destruction (WMD) and bioterrorism, earthquakes and hurricanes, floods and fires, power outages, and personnel reductions may take the primary focus of Business Continuity Planning and Disaster Management, all of these can often result in security and legal issues. Frequently, the disruption caused by legal and security aspects has far-reaching impact beyond an initial event. Unfortunately, these types of incidents occur far too often and are not always handled appropriately. They include:

- Homicide:
  - Co-worker to co-worker
  - Customer to worker
  - Worker to customer
  - Customer to customer
  - Estranged partner to worker
- Robbery:
  - On site with employees (e.g., bank robbery)
  - Off site (e.g., delivery truck)

- Assault:
  - Physical or sexual assault
  - Co-worker to co-worker
  - Customer to worker
  - Worker to customer
  - Customer to customer
  - Estranged partner to worker
- Other criminal activity:
  - Arson
  - Sabotage
  - Embezzlement
  - Destruction of property

While time does not permit us to explore the repercussions that emanate from each of these types of events, it is safe to suggest that each of these situations can result in a wide range of security and liability concerns. As an example, consider the sexual assault of a woman who is staying at a hotel. It is about 9:00 p.m. and the assailant is a well-dressed man who has been sitting in the hotel lobby across from the elevators as if waiting for someone. A woman in her mid-twenties enters the hotel lobby and proceeds to the elevators. As he sees her cross the lobby, he follows her to and off the elevator and then pushes her into the dark room as she is opening the door. He blindfolds her, ties her up, rapes her, and then quietly leaves the room. She is discovered when her muffled screams are heard by other guests in the hallway and they notify the front desk. The front desk calls up to the room and there is no answer. Security is called and they go to the room, hear her calls for help, and proceed to open the door where they find her tied on the bed, partially undressed, beaten and raped.

Certainly this is a trauma for the victim, who is immediately taken to a hospital. The police are called and they have no way of determining whether the assailant is still in the hotel… is he a patron?… an employee? Everyone is considered a suspect. The detectives begin to interview as many guests as possible, as well as staff. The media joins the circus with their vans and news reporters on the streets surrounding the hotel. Imagine the initial impact on the patrons and staff.

Fast forward to two days later. It has been determined that the assailant left the hotel after the assault. The media have had their "involvement" with the incident and the story has fallen off the front page (and even the back page). The victim has been discharged from the hospital. Things are back to business as usual… or are they?

Four weeks later, corporate headquarters of the hotel chain receives a letter from an attorney representing the victim. The attorney indicates that they are bringing charges against the hotel as a result of the sexual assault on his client. They are citing inadequate security and poorly trained staff as the primary reason for the civil suit.

What is the impact at this point on patrons and staff?

Two months later, there is a feature article in the local newspaper about the rate of violent crime in the city's hotels. Specific reference to the sexual assault at the hotel receives significant coverage. The hotel notices that patrons are beginning to ask the front desk personnel about security issues. In addition, there has been a slight decrease in the number of reservations since the article appeared.

Consider the same scenario, but now the assault is against an employee of the hotel. Perhaps one of the housekeeping staff is assaulted while preparing one of the rooms. Or, what if the assailant was an employee of the hotel? Or, what if the victim was an employee and the assailant was an estranged husband?

Does this represent a business interruption? An organizational crisis?

First, one must revisit the definition of "business interruption" from the *Disaster Response Journal* Web site: A **business interruption** is "any event, whether anticipated (i.e., public service strike) or unanticipated (i.e., blackout) which disrupts the normal course of business operations at an organization location."[1] In addition, one must ask what is the **business** of this organization? Is it filling hotel rooms to capacity? Is it the housekeeping and maintenance services? Is it the "customer service" provided by front desk and concierge, parking, landscaping, security personnel? Is it the provision of fine cuisine in the hotel restaurant and lounges? Or, is it something less tangible, such as providing a sense of safety and security for the guests? Is it securing the reputation of the organization? Is it protecting the organization from liability claims? Is it dealing with the social and emotional impacts on the employees of the hotel? One can consider that it is all of the above.

Let's return to the original incident and the receipt of a letter from the victim's attorney. Does this represent a business disruption? The basic services at the hotel continue uninterrupted. The physical premises is untouched. Computers, phones, and other utilities continue to work. Employees continue to come to work on their regular schedule. There is no natural disaster or major power outage. There is no strike, layoff, acquisition, or merger. So what is the disruption?

Think about the impact of the legal proceedings. One can expect the following to occur:

- Corporate legal begins to strategize a response to the letter.
- Part of this strategy is to contact the hotel to review with security and hotel administration what actually transpired.

- The insurance carrier of the company is notified of the potential lawsuit. The carrier begins to plan a response.
- Perhaps there is a need to interview or re-interview employees. If there was an initial interview at the time of the incident, the materials must be read and the individuals re-interviewed. Perhaps some of the employees no longer work at the hotel and efforts are made to relocate them.
- Employees may have been interviewed by the police at the time of the event, then interviewed by hotel security, as well as the hotel legal department and perhaps the insurance carrier's investigator. The ripple effect of these types of interviews is discussed later.
- The media may get wind of the lawsuit and begin to contact the hotel, corporate office, as well as individual employees or guests.

Does this represent a business continuity problem? An organizational crisis?

While the above is a hypothetical situation, albeit based on a real occurrence, consider the following incident and the potential repercussion.

It was reported on the MSNBC Web site that a hospital in Ormond Beach, Florida, had to discipline (including terminating) 25 hospital workers because they did not show up for their scheduled work shifts, claiming the impact of the hurricanes as the reason. According to the article, "Nurses at Florida Hospital–Ormond Memorial were fired for not calling in, not showing up or refusing to work, while others were suspended for not completing a shift or coming late." The hospital drew a lot of "bad press" as a result of this administrative action.

This author spoke with a hospital spokesperson who was able to give more details than the media coverage provided. She claimed that as a healthcare facility, this was part of hospital policy. Further, hospital personnel knew for several days prior to the hurricane that was forecast and to make arrangements for their families. In addition, the individual departments worked with their own personnel to accommodate those who had extreme situations at home. Finally, the hospital made arrangements for 24/7 on-site daycare and set up shelters to house employees' families.

It should also be noted that this hospital is non-union, employs over 2000 people, and that these 25 employees represented about 1 percent. Were it a union workplace, could this have been done? If so, would there have been grievances? Wrongful termination claims?

As with any crisis, there are "lessons learned" or "take away points." Take a moment and speculate as to ways to avoid this type of personnel crisis.

Overview of Violence and Hostility in the Workplace

In the past couple of decades, "workplace violence" has become a familiar term in our lexicon. Vignette 7.1 is an excerpt from a chapter written by this author entitled "Workplace Violence: Protection and Causes" in *Psychopathology in the Workplace* by Thomas and Hersen.[2]

7.1 Workplace Violence: Protection and Causes

Source: Psychopathology in the Workplace by Thomas and Hersen

Now that the world and the workplace have moved into the 21st century, there is increasing awareness of changes in individuals, families, communities, countries, and the workplace. Change leads to stress, and stress produces reactions. The majority of people cope quite well with the stresses of their lives; however, some people become overwhelmed and develop reactions that are maladaptive in nature. While there is mounting concern about workplace violence, it should be understood that this is but one way that people evidence pain, anguish, and suffering. Substance or alcohol abuse, marital/familial, financial or emotional problems, and physical impairments are known to develop if people cannot manage the stresses of their lives. These maladies cause significant turmoil in personal as well as professional lives and place the individual (and the workplace) "at risk" for more severe difficulties.

"Violence in the workplace" has become a familiar phrase in the modern-day employment setting. Reports have been coming fast and furious from a variety of sources citing stories and statistics that increase alarm, anxiety, and apprehension. Statistics are reported in the media that purport a dramatic increase in violence in the workplace. Certainly, one should be concerned about these reports and should make every effort to respond whenever possible. However, this response should be done in an effective and proactive fashion that does not escalate the issue with hype and hysteria! It must be remembered that as tragic as a violent episode may be, it is still a low-frequency occurrence in the workplace.

The National Institute of Occupational Safety and Health reported data indicating that the number of workplace homicides dropped from 929 to 757 between 1980 and 1992. (NIOSH, 2003, ¶ 1 and 2.) Further, this report indicated that 75 percent of these workplace homicides are committed as part of a robbery by an unknown assailant and that only 4–6 percent of homicides in the workplace were committed by co-workers. (NIOSH, 2003, ¶ 11.) Finally, NIOSH and the CDC suggest that there are more than one million nonfatal assaults in the workplace each year.

However, this only represents about 18 percent of the total acts of violence per year in the United States. (OSHA, 2003, ¶ 1–3.) The Department of Justice data reports that between 1993 and 1999, the number of non-fatal assaults decreased by 44 percent while workplace homicides dropped by 39 percent. Eleven percent of these homicides were committed by co-workers, former co-workers or customers (Bureau of Labor Statistics, 2001). There were 639 homicides in the workplace in 2001, down from the 677 homicides that took place at work in 2000 (Bureau of Labor Statistics, 2002).

Although the data may vary as a result of reporting discrepancies and other factors, the numbers indicate that, in fact, the workplace is a relatively safe environment when compared to the streets and homes of America. Compared to feudal systems, slavery, sweatshops, "pre-unionized" factories, and farms, the worker of today is at much less risk of violence, injury, discrimination, or harassment. The last 50 years have seen laws and policies that have improved the quality, comfort, and safety of most workplaces.

While the primary goal of any work organization is to provide business operations, it must be remembered that the Occupational Safety and Health Administration (OSHA) has determined that "Each employer shall furnish to each of his employees employment and a place of employment which are free from recognized hazards that are causing or are likely to cause death or serious physical harm to his employees" 29 U.S.C. 654(a) (OSHA, 2003). In recent years, interpretations of this policy have come to include personal safety. The forward-thinking workplace has instituted workplace violence policies that are similar in scope to sexual harassment policies and protocols.

The goal is to have today's work environment continue to provide an increasing level of safety and security. And while there is no guarantee of 100 percent prevention, there is much that can be done to enhance safety and protection.

During the 1990s, the media (and mental health) attempted to draw attention to workplace violence. However, the focus was on the wrong perpetrator. While articles were written and seminars given about the "disgruntled worker" and how to recognize him or her, it did little to increase a sense of security and safety. In fact, it created a sense of paranoia as people began to become suspicious of fellow workers. Training sessions were developed and rolled out to supervisors about how to recognize the potentially violent individual. The often-cited characteristics are described in Table 7.1. When this author provides training programs, a slide of this material is included and entitled "Interesting, but Unhelpful Information." This is primarily the case because it is too broad, and much of the information will be unknown to the workplace supervisor. Or, as

TABLE 7.1   Often-Cited Characteristics of the Potentially Violent Individual

- 35+ white male
- Familiar with and/or owns weapons
- Likes gun or hunting magazines
- Uses or misuses alcohol or other substances
- Is a loner
- May have a previous history of assaultive behavior
- Complains about work and co-workers
- May have been a victim of early childhood trauma
- May have sustained a head injury
- May have previous history of mental health issues

TABLE 7.2   Average Annual Rate of Homicide in the Workplace by Victim/Perpetrator Relationship: 1992–1999

Relationship to Victim	Average Annual Number	Percentage of Total (%)
Total	897	100
Stranger	753	84
Co-worker, former co-worker	67	7
Customer, client	36	4
Husband	17	2
Wife	—	—
Boyfriend	10	1
Other relationship/acquaintance	14	2

Source: Bureau of Justice Statistics, NCVS.

one police officer stated, "Well, this describes half the guys in our department." And finally, even if we did have a worker who was characterized by the aforementioned qualities, this is not an indicator that he will, in fact, act out in a violent manner. To treat him differently or with increased scrutiny would be akin to racial profiling. "The guy has not done anything wrong but he looks like someone who might... therefore, let's keep an eye on him."

What is now understood is that homicides in the workplace are a true anomaly, and the incidence of co-worker–to–co-worker homicide is a relatively rare occurrence. Table 7.2 describes the average annual rate of

TABLE 7.3 Average Number, Rate, and Percentage of Workplace Violence by Category: 1993–1999

Category	Average Annual Number	Rate per 1000	Percentage of Workplace Violence (%)
All crimes	1,744,200	12.5	100
Homicide	900	0.01	0.1
Rapes/sexual assault	36,500	0.3	2.1
Robbery	70,100	0.5	4
Simple assault	1,311,700	9.4	75.2
Aggravated assault	325,000	2.3	18.6

Source: Bureau of Justice Statistics, NCVS.

homicide in the workplace by victim/perpetrator relationship and also indicates that co-worker–to–co-worker violence is not the primary source of concern. In fact, of the homicides that do take place in the workplace, somewhere around only 5 to 7 percent, are co-worker to co-worker. The same is true for other types of violent behavior. Table 7.3 describes the categories of violent crimes in the workplace between the years 1993 and 1999. These statistics indicate that homicides in the workplace represent less that 1 percent of all the violent crimes that take place in that setting. Sexual assaults and robberies account for an average of 6 percent, while aggravated and simple assaults comprise about 94 percent.

One "fact" widely circulated is that homicide is the second-leading cause of death among women in the workplace. Well, this certainly may give one pause… along with a touch of paranoia. However, if one looks more closely, a woman being killed on the job from any cause is a rare event. Furthermore, most women who are victims of homicide are being killed by people with whom they have been involved romantically, be it a co-worker or non-co-worker. Or, they are victims of another type of crime, such as a robbery or sexual assault, that results in an unplanned murder. For the latter type of situation, improving security tends to be the only solution. For the former, there is much that can be done.

The Cost of Workplace Violence

As indicated previously, homicides are a statistically low-occurring event in the American workplace. However, when they do occur and coupled with the other types of violence, it can be a costly event. The following are some statistics describing the financial impact of business:

- September 1993: a National Safe Workplace Institute study revealed $4.2 billion spent annually. The study estimated that in 1992, 111,000 violent incidents were committed in work environments, resulting in 750 deaths.[3]
- 1995: the Workplace Violence Research Institute reviewed five categories of crime in the workplace: fatalities, rapes, aggravated assaults, threats, or acts of harassment. The results of the research project showed that workplace violence actually resulted in a $36 billion annual loss.[4]

Joanne Sammer wrote in an article, entitled "Combating Workplace Violence" in *Business Finance Mag.com*, that an incident of workplace violence affects a number of variables. She cites the Department of Justice estimate that workplace violence cost companies $6.2 billion in 1992 in lost wages, medical costs, and support costs. Furthermore, she goes on to claim that "[t]he National Council on Compensation Insurance found that companies paid out $126 million in workers' compensation claims for workplace violence in 1995."[5]

As dramatic as these figures may be, they pale in comparison to the legal costs. Sammer continues in her article that "[p]erhaps the biggest potential financial drain on a company is the potential legal liability if the victims of workplace violence or their families pursue civil litigation. Awards in such lawsuits have reached into the millions of dollars in some cases."[6] She also describes the following variables as contributing to the cost of workplace violence:[7]

- Workers' compensation claims for both the injured and any other employees who witnessed or were traumatized by the violent incident
- Increase in medical claims for stress-related illnesses, as well as psychological counseling for all employees after a violent incident
- Management time taken up by managers' involvement in dealing with the press, meetings to help plan the company's reaction to a violent incident, meetings to help get the company back to normal, and other activities tied to a violent incident
- Lost time and absenteeism following a violent incident
- Loss of productivity in the wake of a violent incident
- Litigation costs
- Lost sales, which can occur if a company must close its site for a period of time after a violent incident and if customers cancel orders or postpone purchases in the wake of bad publicity
- Negative publicity, which is difficult to quantify but can have a residual effect on the company

- The company's reactive mode (In the wake of a violent incident, companies tend to go overboard when putting in programs to prevent a recurrence of workplace violence, and these costs can include consultants' time, training programs, enhanced security, and improved safety procedures.)

In summary, an incident of workplace violence has a far-reaching financial impact on an organization when all the cost factors are considered, and as such, should certainly be considered an organizational crisis to avoid.

Interestingly, some types of incidents that wind up costing an organization a large amount of expenditure of resources as well as money are not often considered a violent act. What about destruction of property? Or sabotage? Or civil suits as a result of sexual harassment, wrongful termination, or discrimination?

As reported in an article written by Muarico Valasquez of the Diversity Training Group,[8] the cost of sexual harassment in the public sector reported in 1980 for the previous two years was $189 million. As reported in 1987 for the previous two years, it was $267 million; and in 1994 for the prior two years, it was $327 million. In the private sector, it was estimated that in 1988, some sexual harassment/discrimination claims received more than $15 million per claim in settlement costs. "Today, cumulative costs can come close to $1 billion... for pay-for-pay incongruities, including failure to provide equal pay, offer equal opportunities for promotion, or for not shielding women employees from harassment."

So while all eyes may be on the disgruntled employee or the potential terrorist, many other forms of violence and hostility can be viewed as potential business disruption events.

"Preventing?" Workplace Violence

It is not possible to truly *prevent* acts of hostility and violence. However, there is much that can be done to augment the degree of *protection* by modifying the workplace expectations. This might include:

- Developing policies, procedures, and protocols. It is the opinion of this author that most workplaces are over-policized... there are practically no policies about how to write policies. However, the major problem is that they often stay in a three-ring binder in the HR department or else are jammed into the abundance of paperwork as part of a new hire's orientation. On occasion (usually when deemed necessary to be in compliance with a federal or state mandate), there may be a seminar for employees. Three policies that this author believes are critical to the advancement of positive behavior in the workplace include (1) a workplace hostility policy; (2) a comprehensive job description policy; and (3) a well-developed progress report policy. Table 7.4 provides a sample of a Workplace Hostility Policy.

■ Training first- and second-level supervisors regarding the implementation of these policies and their duties and responsibilities.
■ Educating all employees.
■ Building compliance with workplace policies into regular job descriptions (see "Comprehensive Job Description").

TABLE 7.4   A Sample of a Workplace Hostility Policy

It is the goal of the *ABC Corporation* to provide a physically and emotionally safe work environment. It is imperative that all employees, customers, contractors, and guests, at every level, be treated with the respect and dignity afforded to all humans, regardless of race, nationality, religion, gender, age, sexual preference, or position within the organization. To this end, this policy is being implemented to assist in clarifying the behavioral and procedural expectations.

Definition of Hostility and Violence: No employee shall engage in hostile and/or violent behavior on company property or during any type of company-related activity. *Hostility* refers to any nonphysical forms of harassment, discrimination, and offensive behavior. Examples include but are not limited to: ethnic/sexual/racial jokes; verbal threats or offensive gestures; yelling and/or swearing at an individual; stalking or harassing phone calls, faxes, pager messages. *Violence* is any behavior that results in unwanted physical contact such as hitting, pushing, spitting, biting, or damage to property. Unwanted sexual contact is certainly considered to be hostile and violent behavior. There may be other behaviors that do not fall within these definitions, but also may be considered inappropriate for the workplace.

Definition of Weapons: No employee may bring any firearm, knife, or other form of armament to the workplace or any type of company-related activity. This includes personal lockers, automobiles, etc. No employee may use any object or equipment (e.g.., letter openers, ashtrays, chairs, tools, etc.) as a "weapon" to threaten and/or to inflict bodily harm or damage to property.

Investigation Process: It is expected that any employee experiencing or witnessing this type of behavior will make a report to (personnel, security, human resources, etc.). The alleged incident will be evaluated and investigated by (Safety, Personnel, Human Resources). Also, if a union member is involved, the (union official, steward, etc.) will be notified immediately of the incident and of the investigation. If required, local law enforcement may be contacted. During or after the investigation, there can be no retaliation against any party involved with the incident.

TABLE 7.4   A Sample of a Workplace Hostility Policy (continued)

Pending the results of the full investigation, the individual(s) involved may: (1) be allowed to continue to work; (2) be placed on administrative leave; (3) be referred for a medical/psychological evaluation; (4) be taken into the custody of the law enforcement agency; (5) be transferred; or (6) be placed on some other administrative status.

Confidentiality of Investigation: Every effort will be made to respect the confidentiality of all involved parties; however, this may not always be possible to guarantee, given the nature of the investigation. There may be occasions when other employees/witnesses will be interviewed about the alleged event or the alleged perpetrator's behavior. Should a referral to the EAP or a medical/psychological professional be indicated, a waiver of confidentiality will be requested in order for the investigating party to receive the results of the evaluation. It is understood that the evaluation is not part of the disciplinary process, but is rather an effort to determine the individual's ability to return to work.

Disciplinary Action: Upon completion of the investigation, a decision will be made regarding discipline. Hostile and/or violent behavior may result in disciplinary action, up to and including termination of employment.

The goal of this policy is to prevent incidents from occurring and, those that do, from escalating. Further, it is not the intent of this policy to infringe on the rights of any employee, but rather to ensure courteous behavior. Further, the goal is to do everything possible to ensure a safe work environment for all personnel at all levels. It also should be noted that any parties involved in an alleged incident have the right to seek legal counsel at their own expense.

Please feel free to contact _____ should you have further questions regarding this policy.

Displaced Domestic Violence

In the 1990s, it was estimated that as many as 20 percent of workplace homicides and many of the assaults against women occurred as a result of displaced domestic violence. The woman may have been living in hiding, but the man knew where she worked and went to that place to commit a crime against her… and perhaps other employees. Currently, the numbers vary, but as stated before, many of the assaults and homicides are still perpetrated by an estranged romantic interest. Given this, it is recommended that organizations should include in their workplace violence policy an additional clause that deals with domestic violence and restraining orders. Many women who are victims of violence will not

TABLE 7.5 Sample Language for a Generic Restraining Order Policy

The ABC Corporation makes every effort to maintain a safe work environment. It is also understood that people may have experiences in their personal lives that may place them in vulnerable circumstances. At times, people seek assistance from the police and courts, and they issue a restraining order against someone. Certainly, this is a personal matter and the ABC Corporation has no desire to intrude on one's privacy. However, in an effort to maintain your safety as well as the safety of your co-workers, the following is suggested protocol:

1. If you have a restraining order issued against an individual, please inform (HR, security, etc.).
2. Please bring a copy of the restraining order, which will be kept in a confidential file in case the police need to be called.
3. If possible, please bring a picture of the individual.
4. All efforts will be made to respect and protect your privacy, and only essential personnel will be informed of your situation. Who specifically will be notified will be discussed with you.
5. Please feel free to discuss with HR or your department manager anything that can be done to facilitate your safety and welfare while at work.
6. It is also strongly urged that you seek support services from the EAP (phone number).
7. If your circumstances change and the status of the retraining order is modified, please advise (HR, security).

Once again, it is understood that these may be difficult and private situations. As much as is possible, our goal is to maintain a safe work environment for you and your co-workers. We appreciate your cooperation.

come forward, especially in the workplace. The sense of shame and embarrassment, as well as fear, keeps many victims from disclosing the abuse or seeking services. Including a policy in the Employee Handbook may help those victims come forward, as it demonstrates that they are not alone in their plight. Table 7.5 is a sample of generic language for a restraining order policy.

A Comprehensive Job Description

As the director of an EAP, there have been many times when this author has heard from a supervisor or department head that "You know, Joe is a great worker, but he doesn't get along with the guys in our department."

Or, "Sue does a great job when she works alone at her desk on her computer, but she is always getting into conflicts with others in the office." Or, "When Steve is on, he is really on and gets more work done than most. The problem is that half the time he is not on, calls in sick a lot, takes too much time away from work, and, in general, is a pain in the rear to work with." When consulting with supervisors and department heads, it seems that many do not understand that maintaining behavioral expectations, which include cooperation, communication, and courtesy, is of equal importance as any technical proficiencies.

As the workplace has moved from a manufacturing orientation to one of service and information, it has become increasingly important for people to be able to communicate effectively with both customers and co-workers. However, as the workplace continues to put greater demands on its employees through downsizings, reorganizations, mergers, and such, oftentimes the pressure and stress manifest themselves in the form of confusion and conflict around duties and responsibilities. It is common for workers to become more isolated from each other as a result of the work demand. Lunches in the cafeteria or lounge have been replaced with grabbing a bite at one's desk. Coffee breaks have gone the way of the mythological water cooler as a forum for social "schmoozing" through which workers got to know each other and develop some semblance of a personal relationship. Temporary or contract workers have replaced regular employees, resulting in an ever-shifting dynamic in workplace collaboration. E-mail and voicemail, with their terse and concise format, have replaced direct contact, which allowed for a few moments of social interchange. In sum, as a result of the workplace grinding at an accelerated pace, these and other dynamics have resulted in the social fabric becoming threadbare.

Therefore, it is all the more essential to set up specific behavioral expectations and guidelines to help employees understand that working as a cooperative, communicative, and courteous employee remains a significant component of any job description. So often, job descriptions delineate the technical- and skill-based aspects of employment. So often, organizations have a wide range of company policies and procedures by which employees are expected to abide. (Usually, these policies are communicated only through an employee handbook and/or during the initial orientation.) So often, they are not discussed again unless an individual has made a significant breach of one of them.

Currently, many organizations tolerate a wide range of behaviors that may be considered unsuitable for the workplace. This usually is as a result of it being considered separate and distinct from one's job description and occupational performance. Certainly, as the workplace becomes

TABLE 7.6 Sample Job Description

This position requires that the individual be able to abide by the behavioral expectations (codes of conduct) as delineated in the Employee Handbook. Examples of these behavioral expectations include but are not limited to safety, drug and alcohol, sexual harassment, absenteeism, sick leave policies, etc. [In addition, it is recommended that the job description also include language to this effect:] This position requires that the individual be able to comport him- or herself in an appropriate manner, maintaining courteous and effective interactions and communication with other employees and/or customers. Specifically, this includes but is not limited to:

■ Speaking in a normal tone of voice (no yelling, raised volume, or sarcasm)
■ Refraining from using profane or vulgar language
■ Maintaining respectful personal space and body language
■ Working effectively with others to facilitate the completion of their duties and responsibilities
■ Maintaining suitable dress code and personal hygiene
■ Abiding by company policies
■ Maintaining care and cleanliness of his of her workspace and equipment

increasingly diverse as well as increasingly stressful, there is a need to have very clear guidelines regarding behavioral expectations. Furthermore, employees at all levels need to see that the ability to maintain a certain code of conduct is an essential feature of any job. In addition, including this expectation in a job description would necessitate that supervisors discuss these matters with their supervisees as part of the regular review process. That is, it keeps the "humanistic" qualifications of the job description on a par with the "technological" qualifications.

Presently, most job descriptions focus on technical skills, training, and knowledge and are vaguely worded. Some include an equally indistinctly formulated statement to the effect that the employee shall perform other duties and responsibilities as delineated by his or her supervisor. This common yet obscure wording of a job description can result in further confusion and conflict. Rather, job descriptions should include as essential duties and responsibilities definitive technical and professional skills as well as components such as the ones in Table 7.6.

Some might ask, well if we include this as part of a job description, how does it influence or impact the Americans with Disabilities Act (ADA). The ADA has become an increasingly complex issue since it was first implemented. It is not the goal of this book — nor is there time or space — to develop all of the intricacies, twists, and turns of the ADA policies. However, it would seem that including behavioral expectations (or adherence to Codes

TABLE 7.7 The Ten Commandments for the Workplace

These apply to all employees at all levels.

1. Thou shalt speak in a normal tone of voice (no yelling, raised volume, or sarcasm).
2. Thou shalt refrain from using profane or vulgar language.
3. Thou shalt maintain courteous personal space and body language.
4. Thou shalt work effectively with others to facilitate the completion of their duties and responsibilities.
5. Thou shalt maintain a suitable dress code as designated by the department head or manager. This may include clothing, make-up, jewelry, tattoos, etc.
6. Thou shalt maintain good personal hygiene.
7. Thou shalt maintain care and cleanliness of the workspace and equipment.
8. Thou shalt report to work on time and abide by a specific work schedule.
9. Thou shalt abide by all company policies (i.e., smoking, sexual harassment, drug and alcohol).
10. Thou shalt maintain courtesy and cooperation even in the face of discourtesy.

of Conduct) as part of a job description would actually simplify matters regarding what is and is not a "reasonable accommodation." Further, regardless of disability or protected status, tolerance of the aforementioned behavioral expectations would not be considered a "reasonable accommodation." As an example, there may be an employee who is suffering from bipolar disorder. Extreme moodiness, irritability, emotional hypersensitivity, some paranoid ideation, and hyperactivity can characterize this disorder. It is certainly not a reasonable accommodation to tolerate emotional outbursts, hostile behavior, or disruptions in the workplace. In this case, a reasonable accommodation might be to allow for flex time due to side effects of medication or for therapy appointments, or, perhaps, to change the location of a workspace so as to lessen stimulation and distraction, etc.

In closing, *professionalism* should be defined as having *both* the training, knowledge, skills, and experience to do the work, as well as the capacity to maintain behavioral expectations relevant to the workplace.

When providing workshops, in an effort to be humorous and certainly not to inflict any religious or political over- or undertone, this author discusses the "Ten Commandments of the Workplace"; or the "Workplace Bill of Rights" (right behavior for the workplace)" as presented in Table 7.7.

References

1. www.drj.com, *Disaster Response Journal* Web site.
2. G. Lewis, *Psychopathology in the Workplace,* J. Thomas and M. Hersen, Eds., Brunner Routledge, New York, 2004, pp. 313–331.
3. www.noworkviolence.com/articles/cost_of_workplace_violence.htm.
4. www.noworkviolence.com/articles/cost_of_workplace_violence.htm.
5. www.businessfinancemag.com/channels/riskManagement/article.html?articleID=4365.
6. www.businessfinancemag.com/channels/riskManagement/article.html?articleID=4365.
7. www.businessfinancemag.com/channels/riskManagement/article.html?articleID=4365.
8. www.diversitydtg.com.

Chapter 8

Key Roles Within and Outside the Organization

By now there should be a clear sense that a myriad of incidents may befall and disrupt a work organization and the individuals within that organization. Further, there may be a variety of reactions from the different individuals. Finally, there are stages (phases) as individuals, as well as the organization, travel the journey to re(dis)covery. In any case, the goal is to facilitate the most positive and productive formation of a self-concept or new identity. The personality of the individual is about to change. The culture of the community, country, or workplace is about to shift. How can it be done in a way that does not cause further distress and more pain and suffering? Perhaps, a new type of leadership is required.

The SAFE-T Team

As part of providing a proactive response to business disruption, time and resources must be utilized to develop a team that can set policies, procedures, and protocols. While many organizations already might have an individual or a team, it is usually not sufficiently "wide or deep." Further, the focus is often on getting the business "back on line," with limited priority given to the social and emotional issues. Rather than call it a crisis team, or business continuity team or disaster response team, all of which can provoke anxiety and a reactive orientation, this author prefers the acronym of **SAFE-T team,** which stands for: **Security assessment, Administrative preparedness, Facilitation of resources, Employee services, Training.** This team is composed of key personnel from within the organization: Human Resources, Risk Management, Security, Employee Assistance Program, Legal, representation from supervisors or department heads, representation from labor unions, Information Technology, Maintenance, etc.

In addition, it is important to establish relationships with key organizations outside the workplace that would respond to incidents, including:

- Media
- First responders (police, fire, EMT, hospitals)
- State emergency agencies
- Federal emergency agencies
- Insurance carriers
- Community services: local government, schools, clergy, shelters, counseling centers, etc.

This chapter focuses on developing a team or expanding one that is already in place. In his book, *Blindsided: A Manager's Guide to Catastrophic Incidents in the Workplace,* Bruce Blythe provides a well-organized approach and justification to having what he calls a Crisis Planning Committee (CPC).[1] Whether you call it a CPC, a SAFE-T committee, or a BCP committee, it makes no real difference. What does matter is that it is a committee or group of people who meet together on a regular basis to strategize responses.

Management and Leadership

What exactly do these two terms mean? Are they synonymous, or do they represent two different functions? Do managers lead? Do leaders manage? What does it really matter anyway... how does this all connect to organizational continuity and emergency management?

Henry Mintzberg suggests that since Henri Fayol first began to write about the science of management, four activities describe the role of a manager: (1) planning, (2) organizing, (3) coordinating, and (4) controlling.[2] He continues on to suggest that these activities do not truly begin to describe the role of a manager as much of their time is spent on communicating, building relationships, liaising with outside resources, dealing with inter-employee issues, etc. In other words, so often it is the people issues rather than the professional or technical ones that weigh heavily for a manager.

Put another way, John Kotter writes that managing is about "coping with complexity while leading is coping with change."[3] Put in this author's (Lewis) own terms, leading is looking at the big picture, while managing is dealing with the details. Or, a more pleasant image (at least for this author) is one of sailboat racing. In 1987, this author crewed on a sailboat in the Massachusetts to Bermuda race. Prior to the race, the crew got together many times before the race to talk, eat, practice, and get to know each other and the boat. The goals were to stay safe, to sail hard, and sail to win. The captain (and owner) of the boat worked with the navigator in planning the best course (the big picture). My role was to be on for four hours and then off for fours hours, around the clock. When on duty, I was to "take care of the jib sail." So while the captain led the crew and established where we were going and how we would get there, I among the others had to deal with trimming (managing) the sails. Certainly, as a "trimmer" I would provide some input and information back to the captain, as would the other crew members who were managing other duties and responsibilities. Further, while there was a hierarchy, there was constant communication on board as the conditions changed. I am sure many are wondering how we fared. Well after almost five days, we arrived in Bermuda, very wet, rather ripe, and in first place for our class. This is a classic example of the relationship between leading and managing:

- There was an established relationship between the captain and the crew.
- Each crew member knew his or her duties and responsibilities.
- The captain trusted the crew to do their work without micromanaging it.
- The captain depended on the crew, as the boat could not go without their efforts.
- The captain relied on the crew for input and information that he may not have been aware of.
- The crew members worked with each other (as a cross-functional team) to be sure that all duties were being performed.
- As conditions changed, the entire team provided feedback to both each other and the captain in order to accommodate any changes…maintain the course and complete the race.

There are other metaphors that apply the same logic. Unfortunately, most of them involve sports. Once again, think of a football team that has a captain and team members. The captain or quarterback may call a play, but this is often based on feedback from the team members. The team members then manage their duties depending upon their position. Each position is considered vital and important to the team. After each down, they huddle, provide feedback to each other about the "conditions," and then determine the next play.

Said in a more simplistic yet compelling way by Thomas Teal, "Managing is not a set of mechanical tasks, but a set of human interactions."[4] Teal uses the words "management" and "leadership" interchangeably, and goes on to say that management involves having integrity, which includes taking responsibility, communicating well, keeping promises, and having a good understanding of one's self. Workers will tolerate a boss who may not be technically skilled but who has a great ability to relate to others.

Heifitz and Laurie describe the work of a leader in another way. When work organizations face a crisis of some type, it might be considered an "adaptive challenge." "Adaptive work is required when our deeply held beliefs are challenged." They go on to explain that adaptive work is necessary when the values that were held before are forced to change or become less relevant or irrelevant. The difficult part of adaptive changes is that they "are systemic and have no ready answers." At times that require adaptive changes to respond to the situation, Heifitz and Laurie make three other critical points: (1) "solutions to adaptive challenges reside not in the executive suite, but in the collective intelligence of employees at all levels, often across boundaries"; (2) "adaptive changes are distressing for the people going through it… as new roles relationships, new values and behaviors, and new approaches to work are required"; and (3) often there can be competing perspectives that are all legitimate, yet result in internal turmoil.[5] Once again, think back to the issues of culture as discussed in Chapter 1.

Once again, this is not new information for any of us who have been through any kind of personal or professional crisis. As a country, we have witnessed this since 9/11. We saw Rudy Guiliani respond to the tragedy of New York in a way that catapulted him to "hero" status. (Some may remember that just six months prior to 9/11, he was the subject of great media and political scrutiny involving his marital situation.) However, many believe that his early leadership of New York City as it went through the initial stages of reaction to the event was truly worthy of attention. And, in fact, he has gotten a great deal of that (attention) since then. A consulting company, a book, and at this writing rumor has it that he is being considered for some position in the Bush cabinet.

Fred Fiedler developed a contingency theory of leadership. Summarized quite simply, Fiedler postulated that there were two types of leadership styles: (1) "task oriented" and (2) "relationship oriented." Fiedler further suggested that these leadership orientations were inborn rather than learned. Further, each style is better, depending on the "situational variables." At times of a crisis, he suggested that a take-charge, task-oriented type of leadership is more viable than the relationship-oriented approach. A leader who can manage the big picture, focus on details, and not worry too much about the feelings of the workers (or soldiers) would get better performance from his or her group.

It is my opinion that during the early stages of a crisis or tragedy, this task-oriented approach is critical. However, at later phases, a combination of task-oriented and relationship-oriented leadership is more suitable. Therefore, it is suggested that a team approach to crisis management is best. Some of the team will focus on the operational details (task oriented), while others prioritize the relational orientation.

Norman Bates of Liability Consultants, Inc., is an expert in the field of security and liability issues in the workplace. He is an attorney who is often asked to provide expert testimony for either the plaintiff or defendant (work organization) in cases that involve workplace violence. (I would recommend to the reader a visit to Bates' Web site at www.liabilitycon-sultants.com.) Bates and this author have worked together on several cases. As part of the development of this author's course for the online certificate program in Emergency Management and Organizational Continuity, Bates and I have discussed a wide range of factors of which an organization and its employees must be aware. The following are key elements from our discussions.

Key Points

Investigations and Passive Trauma

With many workplace crises — most discernibly trauma and criminal activities — there is usually a resulting investigation. At times, this may include the organization's security personnel, local and state police, perhaps the FBI, and also the insurance carrier. If civil or criminal litigation is to go forward, further investigation by attorneys might also be included. All of the above may be spread out over months or years. Oftentimes, people express that the crisis or trauma was not nearly as bad as the investigation. Let us remember the concepts of active and passive trauma.

Once again, one way to help mitigate the impact of passive trauma incurred by the investigative process is to do the following:

- Have policies and protocols in place that spell out the nature of the investigation.
- Provide face-to-face information from a supportive resource prior to the investigation to explain the process and expectations.
- Provide support for the individual who is going through the investigation. If not a possibility, then it would be very helpful to have

> someone available to debrief the individual after his or her encounter.
>
> ■ Utilize EAP as a support resource for people who are involved with such investigations.

To Policize... or Not to Policize... That Is the Question

Another area that organizations must be aware of is to have up-to-date policies and procedures. Furthermore, as discussed in other chapters in this book, it is essential that these policies be "rolled out" with training seminars so that all employees have an awareness of them and an understanding of how and when they will be implemented. We discussed at length what Bates refers to as the outdated strategy of "no policy is the best policy." Some lawyers will suggest to an organization that if that organization has a workplace violence policy and there is an incident that goes to litigation (be it civil or criminal), then having a policy can result in the opposing counsel assessing whether (1) it was a comprehensive policy and (2) every detail of the policy was implemented correctly. Therefore, some feel that to have a policy can work against you. In a word, this is *nonsense*. As long as the policy is reasonable and efforts to implement it were reasonable, then it should not splash back on the organization in a harmful way. However, it should be noted that to have any policy that sits in a binder in the Human Resources Department without adequate implementation and training is not a great idea.

Saying You Are Sorry Is Acknowledging Suffering... Not Guilt

Another topic that was discussed was the issue of apologies. There are some lawyers who suggest that it is not a good idea to ever say, "I'm sorry about the accident/injury/robbery/layoff/etc., in which you/your husband/your co-worker was injured/killed/lost his job." Some, from a legal and security perspective, will advise that it is best not to utter these words as they may be construed as an admission of guilt. Some go as far as to suggest that senior management should not attend a funeral of an employee who has died or been killed on the job. Even visiting an injured employee in the hospital might appear too guilt-assuming. So their advice is often to "stonewall," to remain silent, to have no communication with the family except through the lawyers, etc.

Several years ago, this author responded to a workplace trauma in which a regular customer was killed at a sand and gravel company. He had driven his pickup truck into the pit, climbed up on a mountain of gravel, and began to shovel gravel into the bed of his truck. The gravel avalanched down and buried him. The workers ran to the scene and, using their bare hands, tried to find, uncover, and resuscitate him — but to no avail. Owners of the sand and gravel company attended the funeral but were advised by legal counsel not to contact or to communicate directly with the family. Although that regular customer was doing something that was against the rules of the workplace, the family brought a suit against the company, a suit that was later settled out of court. Later, this author did a follow-up on the situation, and was told an interesting story by one of the company owners that is anecdotal and unverified, but nonetheless very interesting. At the end of the settlement meeting, the adult son of the killed customer approached one of the owners of the sand and gravel company and said something akin to this: "We knew that our father was wrong in what he did. If your company had paid a personal condolence call or written a letter… or if there had been an apology as an acknowledgment of the accident, this lawsuit would most likely not have happened."

In discussing this with Bates, we both agreed (legally and emotionally) that apologies do not connote responsibility. Rather, apologizing on behalf of a work organization signifies acknowledgment of a tragedy. It is no different than if one were paying a condolence call to a family who has lost a loved one; when you say something like, "I'm sorry for your loss," or "I'm sorry about the death of your father"; is acknowledging their suffering and sorrow. While some readers might be saying, "I get it; this is rather mundane and you shouldn't be insulting my intelligence with this," it must be understood that the workplace must be able to practice the same degree of acknowledgment and compassion and not have to worry as much about being "LC" (legally correct). If there is an incident in a workplace that results in death, injury, loss of a job, criminal victimization, or any other type of physical or emotional injury, it is imperative for the work organization to provide the same sense of acknowledgment. Even in cases of large-scale layoffs, a personal letter or even a visit from the president of the company, prior to the departure of the personnel, might be a gallant effort toward mitigating some of the potential emotional impact.

In the discussion with Bates, he too has had numerous situations where this is the case. Expressing sympathy or condolences; sending letters, cards, or donations; and attending funerals are an important component of the healing process. In a workplace setting, it is essential for upper management to be available and to communicate directly with the impacted employees. Teal describes in his chapter entitled "The Human Side of Management" the example of William Peace of Westinghouse where 15 employees were to be laid off. Instead of having his subordinates deliver the message, he went before the 15 employees and listened to their complaints, accusations, and upset. He attempted to answer questions directly and understood their feelings. Teal summarizes by saying that by the end of the meeting, the employees came to appreciate the necessity of the decision... even if they did not appreciate being the victims of it.

The point of all of this is to drive home the message that in times of crisis, people need leadership and management at all levels:

- There must be a preexisting relationship among the people.
- There must be established roles and goals for each position.
- The must be policies and protocols in place prior to a crisis.
- There must be practices or drills to see how the plans and protocols work prior to the game or race.
- There must be a method of feedback and communication.
- There must be visibility and availability of leaders.
- Leadership does not mean that one has all the answers, but it does mean that one will listen to the questions.
- Leadership does not necessarily mean that one is charismatic, but a leader must be compassionate.
- Compassion, put very simply, is the ability to acknowledge another's pain.
- Oftentimes, people who rise to the level of leadership have strong egos. However, once one gets there, it is time to back-shelf the ego... a difficult task.
- Do not be afraid to face the victims and to acknowledge their experience by saying you are sorry for what they have to go through.

References

1. B.T. Blythe, *Blindsided: A Manager's Guide to Catastrophic Incidents in the Workplace,* Penguin Group, Toronto, 2002.
2. H. Mintzberg, *The Manager's Job: Folklore and Fact,* Harvard Business School Press, Boston, 1998.
3. J.P. Kotter, *What Managers Really Do,* Harvard Business Review on Leadership, Harvard Business School Press, Boston, 1998, p. 37.
4. T. Teal, *The Human Side of Management,* Harvard Business Review on Leadership, Harvard Business School Press, Boston, 1998, p. 150.
5. R. Heifiz and D. Laurie, *The Work of Leadership,* Harvard Business Review on Leadership, Harvard Business School Press, Boston, 1998, p. 173.

Chapter 9

Employee Services and Programs

By now the message(s) should be clear — but they will be stated once again. An essential component of any BCP, DR, or EM plan is to be sure that care for personnel is given every consideration as a high priority. It should be expected that for some employees, their reactions and ability to return to regular work duties might lag behind the operational aspects of recovery. It will require a team effort to manage the immediate and long-term repercussions. So what can an organization provide for its employees in an effort to mitigate the impact and to ameliorate the situation? Discussion of some of the strategies, concepts, policies, and programs were woven into the content of the preceding chapters. However, at this point, the focus is specifically on services and programs.

Pre-incident Planning
Policies, Protocols, and Plans

1. Your Crisis or SAFE-T team should be sure that the following policies are up-to-date:
    a. Evacuation policies and plans
    b. Workplace hostility policy

      c. Domestic violence/restraining order policy

      d. Sexual harassment policy

      e. All other codes of conduct policies that depend on the nature of the organization (e.g., federal, private, healthcare, educational, etc.)

      f. Physical safety policies

      g. Family shelter in place policy (for emergency management personnel)

2. Once it is determined that all policies are up-to-date, schedule an annual review.

3. Next, each policy should have an established protocol or procedure; that is, how each policy should be implemented. For an example, refer to the workplace violence policy described in an earlier module. Note that within the policy, it also describes the specific steps that are involved.

4. At another time, during training and education sessions, it is important to describe how the procedure would actually take place were an incident to occur.

Employee Data

One of the more complex and confusing issues to manage after a large-scale incident in which people have been forced to evacuate an area is how to maintain communication with them. Oftentimes, the information that an organization has on its employees is outdated, as their addresses and phone numbers may have changed since they originally were hired. Further, Human Resources may have this information but the department heads and managers may not. It was reported to this author that after an incident such as the hurricanes in Florida, many organizations did not know where their workers were, what their health status was, or when they were going to be able to return to work. One anecdote reported by the U.S. Postal Service was that they had to send out postal inspectors to locate some employees whose houses had been seriously damaged.

In addition, employees need to find out the status of the work location. Is it open? Are they to report to a different location? How do they let the workplace know of their status? Immediately after a serious natural disaster, the cell and land line phone utilities often do not work effectively. However, within a day or two, these services are often reestablished. At that time, there should be an "800 number" established by which people can call in to receive information from the organization as well as leave information as to where the employee is located and how to be in communication with them. This communication system should be established and posted as a pre-incident strategy.

Emergency Wallet Cards

While training sessions, posters, and e-mails are helpful in establishing pre-incident plans and strategies, oftentimes they are lost or forgotten at times of serious calamity. It is recommended that the workplace print up and distribute wallet cards to all employees. Pertinent information on these cards might include (1) the "800" information hotline number; (2) evacuation plans and locations; (3) outside support agencies such as state emergency management agencies, Red Cross, EAP, etc.; and (4) any other relevant information. Table 9.1 provides a sample wallet-sized emergency card that is simple to produce and distribute to all employees.

TABLE 9.1   Emergency Card

Work numbers: _____

Police: _____
Fire: _____
Red Cross: _____
Children's numbers: _____

Sig. Other: _____
Other: _____

Other information: _____

- - - - - - - - - - - - - - - - - - - -

Evacuation plan
When requested to do so, please evacuate the building as quickly as possible using stairway X. Proceed to your department meeting area, located at: _____

Be sure to check in with your coordinator: _____

Additional information:

Other responsibilities:

Family Crisis Plans (FCPs)

What has also been learned through experience is that crises often occur unannounced and unplanned. In the case of natural disasters or infrastructure disruptions (power outages, etc.), people might be "trapped" or sheltered at work and unable to get home by usual methods. People might need medications or personal hygiene products. It is recommended that employees put together a small "go kit" that could include these articles as well as any others that may be of benefit. At one training program that this author was conducting, the "go kit" was described and a woman raised her hand and said that she already had a go kit... it was called a "purse."

Families should develop and discuss their own "family continuity plan" (FCP) — what to do in the case of an emergency situation. The following should be included. If parents are not to be home on time, how do they notify each other and the children? What about pets? Carpools? Daycare? What has also been learned is that long-distance phone lines often work better than local lines at times of infrastructure disruption. Therefore, it is suggested that the family designate a family information coordinator who lives in another state. Each member can try to reach this person with their status and messages to one another.

As a personal example of how this would have or could have been helpful, on September 11, 2001, this author was in Alabama (having flown out of Boston on September 10th) conducting a training program; my sister worked in New York City; and my son was living and working in Arlington, Virginia. It took us several days until we were able to come in contact with each other and to determine that all was well.

While it is important to talk about this with children, it is also important to do so in a manner that does not heighten their fear and anxiety. Depending on the age and family circumstances, parents should approach this with some care.

Supervisory Training and Employee Education

This author differentiates between *training* and *education* not in terms of the content of the material presented, but rather that supervisors are expected to implement the policies while employees need only be aware of and abide by them. Often I am asked, "Should we have separate sessions for supervisors and employees?" I suggest, "No, it is important for the employees to hear that the supervisors are now charged with implementing these new policies. In addition, some of these employees may be promoted to supervisors before the next training program."

It is the opinion of this author that first- and second-level supervisors have one of the most difficult jobs. Often, they are promoted from within and frequently wind up supervising workers who were their colleagues just a short while ago. Furthermore, most supervisors receive little to no training as to how to supervise — yet now they are responsible for doing their work as well overseeing that of others. One time, when this author was conducting a supervisory training program and asked what kind of orientation or training they received before they started their new job, one gentlemen said: "On Friday, I was told to wear a tie when I came to work on Monday." Oftentimes, a supervisor is in the position of having little authority but a great deal of responsibility as orders and directives come down from on high. A classic example of this was the supervisor who was told that there was to be a layoff. VP-level administrators had already determined who in the supervisor's department were being let go. The supervisor had to be the one to tell the designated employees.

Even during an ordinary workday, it is a tough spot in which to be. At times of a significant crisis or tragedy, the role of the supervisor becomes even more critical. Even after there may be statements from senior management or services offered by EAP and other departments, it is the supervisor who must manage the day-in-and-day-out tension, turmoil, and toxicity that often develops. It is the supervisor who must interface with employees who are affected by an incident. As described in a previous chapter, as many as 10 to 15 percent of employees may be suffering from some type of emotional condition. After a significant workplace crisis, it could and should be expected that these numbers may rise. Frequently, these problems can manifest themselves as work performance difficulties.

Supervisors need specific and specialized training with respect to how to deal with the aftermath of an organizational continuity problem and its impact on their employees. Specifically:

- How to recognize the troubled employee
- How to communicate with disgruntled employees
- How to improve morale among the workers
- How to be a cheerleader for the team
- How to access other resources to help them (e.g., EAP, HR, other supervisors, etc.)

Evacuation Drills

As discussed in a previous chapter, drills should be practiced on a regular basis and be taken seriously. Specific directions should be posted in hallways as well as on the aforementioned individual emergency wallet cards.

Efforts should be made to prearrange for special populations of personnel, such as the physically handicapped, elderly, foreign speaking, and intellectually or mentally disabled. They may need to have someone assigned to them during a time of evacuation and crisis.

Employee Services and Interventions

Comprehensive Employee Assistance Program (EAP)

As we enter the twenty-first century, the majority of companies in the United States now have an employee assistance program (EAP). However, these programs are still not well understood by many within the workplace. Furthermore, many EAPs are not providing the full complement of services that they advertise; or, many companies are not availing themselves of these services if they are provided.

The establishment of EAPs first began in the 1970s. By then, many American workers were bringing their 1960s-era recreational drug and alcohol use into adult life and adult work. Prior to this time, there were two primary methods of dealing with an employee who had a substance abuse problem: ignore them or fire them. It was also the era of the "three martini lunch" and a wide range of other behaviors that were fairly well tolerated. As the late 1970s came into focus, it became more evident that alcohol was becoming a growing problem in the workplace that could no longer be denied. In addition, the cost connected with either the strategy of ignoring or firing wound up costing the employer on many levels. The informal grass-roots efforts of getting people into rehab or treatment or to Alcoholics Anonymous meetings became more formalized. During the 1980s and 1990s, precipitated by transportation accidents such as the Exxon Valdez, workplaces began developing drug and alcohol policies, drug testing, and supervisory training. EAPs became a mainstay as a resource for evaluations and referral of employees. For some companies, this is where the EAP began and ended. For most, the programs developed a "broadbrush" orientation to assisting employees with a variety of difficulties ranging from alcohol to anxiety, from drugs to depression. They began to serve not only the employee, but also his or her family members, as it was recognized that an impaired family member could be a significant source of stress to an employee.

As time went on, the EAP became an educational resource for a myriad of health issues, providing training programs on stress management, smoking cessation, healthy eating, and other "wellness programs." Yet, even then (i.e., the mid-1990s), they were still seen as primarily a "clinical" service rather than a consultative one.

Another service that came to reside under the domain of the EAP was critical incident stress debriefings (CSIDs). While this topic is discussed in greater detail later in this chapter, CISDs (or, more appropriately labeled, psychological debriefings) rapidly became a service that the EAP would provide to an organization that had experienced some significant traumatic event in the workplace, such as the death of or injury to employees. Still, the EAP was seen as providing a "clinical" service.

It has been and remains the opinion of this author that clinical services are just one component of a comprehensive EAP. EAPs should be viewed as a consultation resource that can be extremely useful in the development of policies and protocols. Working with the Human Resources, Legal, Security, Risk Management, Occupational Health departments, the EAP should be part of any SAFE-T or Crisis Team.

Be Sure That Your EAP Is a Right Fit for Your Company

Many managed care and disability insurance carriers began to offer EAPs in the 1990s. These were often national programs that had a list of providers and would outsource the employee to a provider in their network. While this may serve to be useful for the individual employee, there is often little in the way of direct contact between the EAP and the client organization. Often, this author receives requests from an EAP to do some training or to respond to a critical incident. So imagine, if one will, walking into a workplace with no preexisting relationship and providing a canned presentation that was designed by someone in the EAP's training department. With respect to consultation, it can often be handled in the same manner. The call goes out to the EAP and then the EAP finds someone nearby to provide the consultation service. From this author's perspective, this is not the best dynamic to gain a relationship with the client organization or to provide the best quality of service. However, many EAPs do "outsource" their crisis intervention work. This may be a suitable methodology because these crisis networks at least make an effort to be sure that the individual who is responding to the incident has had suitable training and experience.

On the other side, a company might have an "internal EAP." This is a program in which the EAP provider is an employee of the company and provides EAP services on-site and primarily to its own organization.

It is strongly recommended that the EAP should fit the company. If you are a local work organization, get a local EAP; regional, get a regional EAP; national, go national. If you are a small local company and contract with a national provider because it can deliver a lower cost, do not expect a great level of utilization or service.

Be it an internal or external program, there are several features that should be available to a client organization for it to be considered a comprehensive program, including:

- Confidential clinical assessment and referral
- Education and training seminars
- Supervisory training
- Psychological debriefings
- Consultation to administrative departments
- Managing fitness for duty evaluations

When teaching my course on The Social and Psychological Impact of Workplace Disruption, one of the assignments is to interview the EAP to determine what services it is prepared to provide in times of crisis. The feedback has varied from, "I didn't know that we had an EAP," to "The EAP was an 800 number and only does telephonic counseling," to "My EAP had a wide variety of services that they could offer." It is strongly recommended that readers "check out" if their company has an EAP and, if so, what it can do.

Information Is the Lifeblood during a Crisis

One of the primary needs during any type of crisis is that people require information. As discussed in previous chapters, if one thinks of a work organization as a living system, then information is the blood that circulates within the departments (organ systems), providing the necessary nutrients to keep the system functioning. As is the case during and after surgery, a patient may need multiple transfusions to survive. The same holds true for a work organization; it is better to have too much information rather than a lack thereof. However, because information is fluid, it may be inaccurate. This can be as damaging as giving a patient a transfusion with the wrong blood type. Therefore, there is a need to have the information vetted and regularly updated as conditions and circumstances modify. This author has seen and suggests the following:

- An administrative person should be designated as the information coordinator. Depending on the situation, this role could switch from HR to Legal to Security, etc.; however, the individual(s) should be someone who is facile dealing with distraught and emotional workers and family members.
- During the initial phase, the aforementioned "one-dial" system of sending messages should be utilized on a regular basis to keep people updated.

- As discussed, an "800" number with a prerecorded message should be set up (prior to an incident) and be posted for all employees. It should be updated every one to two hours with a time acknowledgment: "This report is issued at 10 a.m. on Wednesday the 15th of 2004…." As was also described, this number should include a capacity for employees to leave information about their individual situations.
- The same information should be posted on the company Web site.
- A FAQ (frequently asked questions) sheet should be posted on the Web site.
- Teleconferences, videotaped messages, and informational meetings should be conducted on a regular basis as people need face-to-face contact with administration.
- Often, the tendency is for supervisory personnel to isolate, and this must be countered with an increase in visibility and availability…walking around making contact with employees.
- All employees should receive a wallet-sized card (see Table 9.1) that includes the following information:
  - In the case of an evacuation, a reminder to return to their desk to retrieve their personal belongings (if possible)
  - The evacuation path and outside meeting destination
  - What to do once they are outside
  - The 800 information hotline
  - Outside support agencies: state emergency management, Red Cross, EAP, etc.
  - Company Web site and where information is posted

Information systems must have consistency, redundancy, frequency, circularity, and continuity:

- *Consistency.* The information passed along must be consistent from source to source. This requires interdepartment and centralized communication.
- *Redundancy.* There should be a variety of sources by which people are able to access information. E-mails, Web site postings, "800" numbers with a recorded message, face-to-face informal information sessions, newsletters, etc., are all methods to disseminate information.
- *Frequency.* During crises, information becomes outdated rather quickly. Therefore, it is important to keep the outgoing information updated and sent out regularly.
- *Circularity.* The passing along of information cannot be done in a vacuum or based on guessing what the workers might want to know. There must be a method by which the concerns and questions can come in and then consistent information be given out.

■ *Continuity.* Oftentimes, there is a flurry of outgoing information early on during a crisis. Then, it often drops off rather rapidly. As discussed previously, crises tend to roll on for a while and people may need different types of information from stage to stage and over an extended period of time.

It is essential to remember to include communications with each of the following groups and to assume that it will find its way to the media:

- Employees
- Customers
- Government and community leaders
- Families of employees
- Insurance companies and lawyers
- Media (press releases)

While each group may have the message customized to the specific group, they should all have about same consistency.

Media Management

"Media management" seems like an oxymoron. The media is often a mixed blessing in times of distress and destruction. They usually arrive like a swarm of locusts, covering anything in their path, intrusively filming the event, and even interviewing victims at the height of their emotional distress. In recent years, news coverage has moved into a 24/7 format and this author has serious concerns with respect to the potential exploitation of victims and the validity of reporting. Be that as it may, it is suggested that efforts be made to see the media as a viable and valuable resource to facilitate the recovery process. By designating someone in the workplace as the media liaison, that individual can form relationships with the print and electronic media prior to an incident. Then, if an unfortunate incident were to befall the workplace, there is already an established protocol for generating press releases and informational articles. Often, the media may be looking for some follow-up articles that may be of interest to the general public. This author has been asked to provide background information to the media about topics such as emotional reactions to crises, how to handle children after a parent has been laid off, the impact of workplace violence, etc.

While freedom of speech and freedom of the press are two of the basic tenets of this country, it is the recommendation of this author that a company develop a media policy that suggests to employees that they

TABLE 9.2   Recommended Media Policy Language

While the ABC Corporation understands that any employee has the right to speak to the media, the following recommendations are made with respect to incidents involving company matters.

Certainly, any operational and business matters deserve the utmost confidentiality and privacy and therefore no one should divulge any company information to the media including their opinions or speculations.

Unfortunately, there may be times when a workplace is faced with an incident such as an accident, fire, robbery or other criminal activity, natural disaster, layoff, or other type of crisis, and the media may respond and want information or reactions from employees. While it is understood that any employee has the right to talk to the media, it is strongly recommended that all inquiries (either on-site or if they call your home) be directed to our media liaison, Ms. Smith.

Please understand that these policies and protocols are suggested in an effort to protect you as well as the company from information (or misinformation) falling into the wrong hands or being used in an inappropriate manner.

If you have any further questions regarding these policies, please feel free to contact our media liaison directly.

Thank you for your cooperation.

not speak directly to the media, but rather that they refer inquiries to the media liaison. Table 9.2 provides a sample media management policy.

People who are upset or in a heightened emotional state might inadvertently discuss or disclose information that they otherwise would not. They might respond with anger or fear that could be used or misused in some provocative manner. This is not suggesting a gag order, but rather a recommendation that is designed to protect the employees as well as the workplace and to maintain an appropriate boundary for the media. This is recommended to avoid the situation where a reporter shoves a microphone into an employee's face and generates an out-of-context sound bite that might wind up on the news that evening. The next day, the employee might be in the uncomfortable position of having to explain why he said what he said. A media liaison who has received training can do a better and more consistent job of managing the information that is given to the public after an incident. If they have a preexisting relationship with the media, then expectations and guidelines will have been determined prior to the incident.

If there is an incident to which the media will respond, it is of critical importance to meet first with the police and fire departments to determine

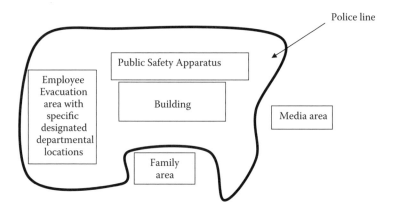

FIGURE 9.1   Evacuation plan setup.

where they need to have access. If anyone has been to a serious incident, it usually seems like chaos prevails. Police feel that the fire apparatus is in the way, and vice versa. The media is often monitoring the emergency communications and also shows up. A crisis team should have a large map that delineates where the media should be directed. It is recommended that the media be placed away from where the employees are gathering if there is an evacuation. Further, as the reports from the media go out over the local news, family members often will respond by going to the scene. Usually, there is a police line and the family members are kept outside because it is considered a crime scene. It is strongly recommended that there be a family liaison person who responds to the family area to be available to them as they arrive at the scene.

Refer to Figure 9.1, a schematic of a simple evacuation plan that includes areas for family and media personnel. This should be taken in the manner in which it is meant — a simple plan. Yet, many organizations do not even include something as simple as this in their evacuation policies. These schematics should be posted throughout the workplace.

Crisis Intervention

Intuitively and anecdotally, it is well established that the practice of providing crisis intervention to people who have experienced a trauma or tragedy can be of great benefit. After the Coconut Grove fire in Boston in 1940, Eric Lindemann wrote his oft-cited work on crisis intervention, extolling the need for an immediate response, an allowance for the expression of grief, and a here-and-now problem-solving focus.[1] Kardiner and Spiegel worked with combatants of World War II and developed the

"PIE" model, where soldiers with "shell shock" were treated within close Proximity of the battle, Immediately, and with the Expectation that they would return to battle readiness and to the front line. Later they added Brevity, suggesting that treatment should be for no longer than ten days.[2] Since these early works, the fields of psychiatry and psychology have embraced the concept that the provision of a brief, problem-oriented, "normalizing" treatment strategy is of great efficacy with victims of trauma. More recently, the methodology has taken on a multi-modal approach that embraces talking, medication, body work (massage, yoga, Reiki, etc.), and spirituality.

Group Psychological Debriefings

Historical Event Reconstruction Debriefing (HERD)

Brigadier General S.L.A. Marshall was the chief U.S. Army historian in World War II, Korea, and Viet Nam. He developed the method of conducting interviews with the surviving members of small units in the field soon after the battles.[3] While these group sessions were primarily for the purpose of gathering historical facts, he found that these historical debriefings, when properly conducted, were also very beneficial to the units themselves. The process repaired and strengthened unit cohesion and readiness to return to battle. Marshall described the HERD protocol as having the following characteristics:

- Clearly stated outline of aim of the discussion
- Respect for individual's experience
- Suspension of judgment
- Suspension of rank
- Tolerance for different perspectives as to what occurred
- Sequential exposition of the event
- Emotional response was accommodated but not emphasized
- Confidentiality could not be guaranteed
- There was no time limit and often these groups would meet for several days

Psychological Debriefings

In the 1980s, Mitchell took notice of what was known but unspoken: people in public safety jobs dealt with a unique type of stress. He coined the phrase "critical incident," referring to the types of situations that police and firefighters respond to in which people are hurt, maimed, killed, assaulted, vandalized, etc.[3] He described the impact of working in these careers and experiencing the exposure to the victimized as "critical incident stress." He developed a structured group intervention that he labeled a "critical incident stress debriefing" (CISD), where the affected public safety personnel would meet and describe the event and their reactions to it. The goals of the intervention were to acknowledge the experiences of each member, to allow for the expression of emotions, and to be supportive and nonjudgmental of each other. In general, these meetings were facilitated by other police officers and firefighters who had received training in leading CISDs. Special attention was devoted to being sure that they remained confidential.

Within a decade, public safety embraced the concept and many were trained in implementing debriefings. The concept spread beyond public safety, and debriefings were offered in public and private work settings when incidents occurred. (In 1994, this author's first book, *Critical Incident Stress and Trauma in the Workplace,* was published.[4]) In recent years, there has been some controversy surrounding the efficacy of debriefings. Vignette 9.1 is the original of an article that was published in the *Journal of Employee Assistance* (Vol. 32, No. 1, first quarter 2004) covering the major points of the controversy.

9.1 Thoughts on the Psychological Debriefing Controversy

Source: Journal of Employee Assistance, 32(1), first quarter 2004.

Over the past several years, there has been growing debate over the efficacy of psychological debriefings. This author addressed some of the pertinent issues in an article published in *Behavioral Health Management,* July 2002.[1] While controversy and examination are good and often generate useful discussion and an exercise in "lessons learned," the recent *trashing* of debriefings as a viable service seems to be a bit reactionary, unjustified, and founded on inadequate and poorly designed research.

Part of the problem is that somewhere along the line, someone may have said or inferred that debriefings prevent PTSD. That is certainly a naïve notion. Most mental health professionals understand that if an individual sustains an experience resulting in a *bona fide* diagnosis of PTSD, a single intervention of any type is not enough to manage the disorder. Usually, a multimodal approach of talk therapy in combination with medication and other interventions such as EMDR, hypnosis, cognitive behavioral therapy, exercise, support groups, etc., is required to deal with the disorder over an extended period of time.

Some "experts" have made remarkable assertions that debriefings may, in fact, cause PTSD. As reported in the *Crisis Management Quarterly* (Summer 2003): "Possibly because CISDs focus on re-hashing and re-telling upsetting events, a diagnosis of PTSD could be more likely. As a result, a negative outcome, supported by the growing body of reputable research, could provide the basis for lawsuits alleging negligence in an organization's crisis response."[2] There is little question that a debriefing must be more than "rehashing and retelling upsetting events," or it is of limited benefit. Yet, more and more institutions are dismissing the interventions based on faulty studies and a naïve misconception. "The American Red Cross and the American Psychological Association have stated in a draft conclusion that post-trauma debriefings have not been shown to prevent later difficulties and may even cause problems to become entrenched or more severe over time." An equally valid hypothesis may be that (since debriefings are voluntary) only those who were truly upset about the incident may have chosen to attend the debriefing and may have developed PTSD regardless of their participation in the debriefing. Further, there may have been a greater number of "upset" people who went on to develop PTSD had they not attended the intervention. Or, perhaps, some people were able to recognize the symptoms of PTSD as a result of being at the debriefing and availing themselves of further services. We will never know, because anyone who understands research design is aware of the impact of self-selection bias on statistical results. Other studies make reference to the negative findings of the Cochrane Review and hold it as the benchmark research.[3] The Cochrane Review looked at a diverse range of studies of individuals from many different facilities that "received individual crisis intervention bearing little resemblance to psychological debriefing and at times applied to situations where major stress reactions are not expected."[4] Further, these interventions were provided by a diverse group of practitioners without the benefit of a specific model. Comparing the Cochrane Review to debriefings is an "apples with oranges" proposition. The problems with the Cochrane Review are not limited to this one report. As stated in "Psychological Debriefing" by the British Psychological Society, "There are serious flaws in many of the studies that evaluate debriefing. Several fail to define debriefing, describe the protocol used or the training of the debriefers."[5] Once again, there must be a valid research design before we decimate an intervention that (at least) has a fair amount of anecdotal support.

Another possible reason why there may be controversy about debriefings is that some prescribe a rather rigid intervention structure. While having a theoretical framework or intervention model is important, it is impossible to have a one-size-fits-all approach to psychological debriefings. As examples, this author has always felt that "CISD" applies only to those crisis care professionals who are in the forefront of crisis, trauma, and disaster response, or who deal directly with the victims of such incidents: police, fire, EMTs, crisis workers, clergy, mental health, Red Cross, etc. It is part of their career... for which they are trained, equipped, and respond as a team. When a tragedy befalls a regular workplace, this is <u>not</u> a *critical incident*, nor does one provide a CISD. Rather, this is *trauma in the workplace,* with far more dramatic impact on those involved because: (a) it involves a co-worker with whom they may have had a personal relationship; (b) the true "first responders" are co-workers; (c) they have little to no formal training; (d) they had no warning; (e) they must go back to work and revisit the scene; (f) they have not developed the "emotional calluses" or defense structure that professional crisis care providers have developed over the years of doing the job. Therefore, one cannot compare services delivered to crisis care professionals (CISM) with those of workplace trauma victims. Thus, the possibility of a more dramatic impact, a higher incidence of PTSD and a need for more robust intervention should be expected and understood.[6] Further, there are many occasions where this author has been called to provide services to a workplace after the death of an employee that has taken place outside of work and therefore not witnessed/experienced by employees. This, too, is not a CISD, nor a workplace trauma debriefing. This is designated as *meeting to talk about the death of ___.* This could apply to suicides, sudden tragic deaths, succumbing to a long-term illness. One may imagine that the psychological agendas of the participants of each type of incident would be very different. Therefore, the facilitators would need to orient the discussion to meet the specific character of the situation, as well as the demographics of the participants. In fact, when not working with paramilitary organizations such as police, fire, hospitals, etc., this author has moved away from the term "debriefing" and, instead, describes the intervention in regular layperson's terms such as "meeting," "discussion," "get together to talk about the...," etc. Certainly, the term "CISD" should not apply to any type of intervention around an administrative crisis such as a downsizing/layoff, relocation, removal of CEO, etc. And finally, it is difficult to know exactly what the participants have been told about the upcoming meeting. This author has discovered that by now, most police, fire, and hospital professionals have an understanding of CISM and debriefings. However, in a workplace trauma, many come to the debriefing/meeting with little to no true understanding of what it is about. Therefore, this may lead to a less than positive experience for some. In order to get all on the same playing field and to mitigate some of the inconsistency in communication about the meeting, this author drafts up a statement and faxes/emails it to the workplace liaison so it can be utilized as part of the "invitation" to potential participants. Further, there are handout materials for the participants to take with them that are pertinent to the situation, be it a trauma in the workplace, suicide at home, layoff, etc. Most importantly, this material indicates that the debriefing is only one of many techniques or services to help if the reactions persist.

Another reason why the efficacy of debriefings may be called into question is that after a debriefing, the administrative personnel may expect that "all is well"… "people should be back on track." Or, query a week later, "How come people are still upset? They had a debriefing, didn't they?" When called to a workplace to provide an intervention, we must be careful not to collude with their denial or lack of understanding. This means that, in addition to a debriefing, one must provide good consultation to the workplace and help management appreciate that their employees might require more than a single meeting.

We must stop using 9/11 as the yardstick by which to measure the efficacy of any interventions. 9/11 was "so over the top" of our experience that to draw any inference regarding psychological services is only speculation. Certainly, it is understandable that for an event of that magnitude, a single debriefing of the police, fire, survivors, etc., may serve as little more than a well-intentioned "spit in the bucket." For many people who experience a dramatic trauma, a single intervention of any type may not be enough to mitigate their symptoms and alleviate their suffering. However, the question is not whether the debriefing is useless, but rather what other services should be available? The goal of trauma support is to have a "trauma toolbox" that is both wide and deep (and utilized by experienced practitioners). Further, that as an initial proactive intervention, the debriefing may serve to facilitate the access to further services for those in need.

Let us now talk about training. As a psychologist for more than 25 years and doing this work for more than 17, this author believes that working with groups of people who have experienced a major trauma should be considered an expertise that requires training, experience, consultation, staying current with the literature, etc. A one- or two-day workshop is a good start, but not sufficient for people who are serious about becoming or remaining proficient in this specific field. And finally, while the "peer support" model may be sufficient for police, fire, hospital, etc. employees, it is not the recommendation that they be the ones to provide services to other types of employment settings.

There are many issues that must be taken into account, such as type of incident, demographics of the victims, demographics of the participants, training and supervision of facilitators, documentation, management consultation, post-debriefing follow-up, etc. Then, perhaps, a well-founded research design that takes into account controlling incident demographics, utilizing a specific model, random assignment of participants to treatment and non-treatment groups, pre-morbid history and personal variables of the participants, training and experience of facilitators and long-term follow-up with a consistent method, would provide viable data. Since humans are not mice in a lab, any qualified research that measures the benefit of mental health interventions is always fraught with some design limitations. Therefore, one must be careful not to rely too heavily on the "latest research." In the words of Albert Einstein, "Not everything that counts can be counted. Not everything that can be counted counts."

References

For a comprehensive review of the literature on the wide range of issues related to psychological debriefings, "Psychological Debriefing," by the British Psychological Society (www.bps.org.uk/documents/Rep12.pdf) is strongly recommended by this author.

1. G. Lewis, Post-Crisis Stress Debriefings: More Harm than Good?, *Behavioral Health Management,* 22(4), 22–25, August 2002.
2. A. Tennyson, When Doing the Right Thing Might Be Wrong, *Crisis Management Quarterly,* V, 32, Summer 2003.
3. S. Wessely, S. Rose, and J. Bisson, A systemic review of brief psychological interventions (debriefing) for treatment of immediate trauma related symptoms and the prevention of post-traumatic stress disorder. The Cochrane Library — 1998, Issue 4, 1998 and 2001.
4. British Psychological Society, Psychological Debriefing, May 2002, www.bps.org.uk/documents/Rep12.pdf.5.British Psychological Society, Psychological Debriefing, May 2002, www.bps.org.uk/documents/Rep12.pdf.
5. Ibid.
6. G. Lewis, *Critical Incident Stress and Trauma in the Workplace,* Accelerated Development, Taylor & Francis, Philadelphia, PA, 1994.

While sufficient objective research has not been conducted, the anecdotal feedback from people participating in psychological debriefings is generally quite positive. Over the years, this author has conducted more than 300 debriefings for a wide range of incidents to an equally diverse group of organizations. The model that this author developed has some significant differences from the "Mitchell model" that was originally designed for public safety personnel. While these differences are not discussed in this book, it is important to understand if the providers of these services have received specific training and, if so, with what model. Further, it is important to know of the level of experience of the facilitator(s). However, the provision of group and individual debriefings should be a highly utilized component of any crisis or disaster response during the support phase. In addition, it should be understood that debriefings are generally utilized during the initial post-incident phases (survival and support) and should not be viewed as a stand-alone intervention. Rather, they should be seen as an integral component of a comprehensive intervention strategy and that other services will be of benefit at later phases. As indicated previously, acknowledgment and information are such critical components to recovery after a disruptive incident. Debriefings may serve several benefits, including (1) a coming together as a group to acknowledge the incident; (2) acknowledgment from management; (3) a "normalizing" process (discovering that many people may be having the same reactions as you); and (4) the receipt of information. Vignettes 9.2 through 9.4 are samples of printouts that this author gives

9.2 An Introduction to Psychological Debriefings

In recent years there has been much focus on the effects of traumatic events on individuals. Oftentimes, people have dramatic reactions to these extraordinary events that may leave them feeling overwhelmed and upset. When a significant crisis occurs, the individuals involved may benefit from an opportunity to talk about the experience as a group. For that reason, "critical incident debriefings," "trauma debriefings," and "psychological first-aid services" have been promoted as a method to help healing and resolution.

A debriefing is a meeting that generally includes only the affected individuals and a facilitator whose responsibility is to provide a structure and organization to the meeting. This meeting is *not* group therapy, but rather is described as a "psycho-educational" experience. The discussion focuses primarily on the traumatic event and its effects on the individuals, not on personal relationships, personality problems, or professional conflicts. Most importantly, it is neither a critique or investigation of what occurred, nor is it a courtroom to determine guilt or innocence.

The following are some guidelines about today's meeting:

1. Although you may be encouraged to participate, no one will be forced to talk.
2. I will maintain confidentiality about the meeting. Often, an organization wishes to receive some *general* feedback about the session. If this is the case, I will discuss this with all of you.
3. Talking about the event that you have been through is an important part of the recovery process. Preferably, you should talk to family members or "significant others" about the debriefing. If you do so, please protect the privacy of the other participants.
4. Feel free to move around freely to get food and beverages or to go to the bathroom. If you do leave the room, please let me know if you will not be returning.
5. The debriefing goes through certain phases. After going over these guidelines, we will start by asking the participants to "paint the picture" by describing the event from their perspective. Usually, we try to go in sequence or chronological order as to how the event transpired. I may ask you questions and you may go into as much or as little detail as you wish.
6. After that, I will ask you to describe your reactions at the time of the event and since then. You may want to refer to the other handout to see the "menu" of common reactions to traumatic events.
7. Throughout the debriefing, feel free to ask questions, and I will attempt to answer them as best as I can.
8. Usually, these types of meetings last between one and two hours.

9. There will be follow-up telephone contact with each of you a week or two after this meeting.

Not everyone experiences the same reactions to difficult situations. The recovery process takes time.

---

to the participants of psychological debriefings. Each participant will receive two of the handouts. One of the differences of this model of conducting debriefings is that this author differentiates between interventions with safety personnel (police, fire, rescue, hospitals, etc.), referring to them as critical incident debriefings. These professionals are providing services as part of their jobs and may have a different psychological agenda to a "bad" incident. The rescue professionals receive the handouts in Vignettes 9.2 and 9.3. Regular employees who have experienced a tragedy and may have witnessed traumatic injuries, etc., to colleagues and friends, will respond to this differently (and usually more dramatically) than rescue personnel. If the victims are regular employees of a work setting that has experienced a significant tragedy or crisis, they receive the material in Vignettes 9.2 and 9.4. While the materials in Vignettes 9.3 and 9.4 are similar in scope, one can see that there is a different orientation to each. These printed handouts also serve to provide information and support to family members as well as employees who may not have attended the debriefing.

Another form that is often utilized is a brief, confidential evaluation form through which the participants can provide feedback (see Table 9.3). The results of this form can be summarized and given to management while retaining the confidentiality of the individual participants.

Family Services

After a dramatic workplace crisis, there is a ripple effect with respect to the impact — certainly, the workplace and its customers, then the workers' families, then collateral work organizations. For now we only focus on family concerns. A workplace facing a BC problem must consider the impact on them. Usually, what is required is information and EAP services. At one national EAP conference, this author was talking to a colleague who happened to be an internal provider at a large company in the midwestern part of the United States. He described that during a large flood that damaged many workers' personal properties, in addition to providing individual counseling and group debriefings, the EAP helped people complete homeowner insurance claim forms as part of their services. In another example, arrangements were made for insurance companies to be available at the workplace to help employees complete the forms.

TABLE 9.3   Debriefing Evaluation Form

Please respond to the following statement using a 1–10 rating scale, where 1 indicates a negative response and 10 a positive response.

___ I was looking forward to the debriefing.
___ I felt that the debriefing was a worthwhile experience.
___ I felt free to express my thoughts/feelings.
___ I trusted the privacy___ and confidentiality___. (two ratings)
___ The facilitator(s) did a good job of organizing the meeting and keeping it going and relatively comfortable.
___ I think we should have these types of meetings when there are other incidents such as this one.
___ This meeting was helpful to me in dealing with this difficult event and understanding my and others' reactions.

Please feel free to write any other comments regarding the psychological debriefing.

While your individual responses to this evaluation will remain confidential, the total responses may be calculated and reported back to management personnel.

9.3 Introduction to Critical Incident Stress Management (CISM)

In recent years, an increasing amount of research has been devoted to the impact on professionals who respond and provide services to the victims of trauma and crisis. Dr. Jeff Mitchell initially described a "critical incident" as an event that can be considered extraordinary and, therefore, may produce significant reactions in the intervening personnel. Critical incident reactions (CIRs) often are a common reaction of an average person to an extremely stressful situation. A CIR can manifest itself as a physical, cognitive, or emotional response that may be experienced almost immediately or may be delayed days, weeks, or months.

The following is a brief summary of (1) the types of situations that may result in CIRs; (2) the signs and symptoms of CIRs; and (3) the strategies and interventions that are helpful to individuals with CIRs.

Most professionals manage the stress of their career quite well on their own. However, it is understood that people who understand the effects of CIR, and have a process by which to discuss the events and their reactions, often speed up the recovery process, stay healthier, remain more productive on the job, and have less disruption in their personal lives.

Types of Situations That Might Result in CIR

Single Victim Incident(s)	Multi-casualty/High Intensity/ Long Duration
Line-of-duty death of fellow-professional	Catastrophic natural event (earthquake, hurricane, etc.)
Death of a child	Transportation accidents
Serious injury of a child	Fires
Death of adult	Hostage taking
Threat of violence or injury to ESP	Terrorist actions
Inability to intervene or perform duties	Rescue operations
Injury to fellow professional	Long duration incidents
Suicide	

Signs and Symptoms of CIR

Physical	Cognitive	Emotional	
Fatigue	Memory impairment	Anxiety	Grief
Nausea	Anomia (word loss)	Fear	Frustration
Muscle tremors	Difficulty with decision making	Irritability	Hopelessness
Sweating/chills	Mental confusion	Guilt	Dizziness
Startle responses	Intrusive thoughts/ visions	Feeling remote and numb	
		Sleep disturbance/ nightmares	
		Intrusive thoughts/visions	

Strategies and Interventions to Help with CIR

Critical Incidents should be considered "emotional haz mat."
- Education about CISM as part of training
- Availability of CIS debriefings
- Regular exercise, good diet
- Open attitude within the department or agency to discuss reactions
- Maintain good social network
- Limit alcohol and other controlled substances
- Try to eat regularly even if appetite is disturbed
- If sleep is disturbed, do not toss and turn in bed. Read, watch TV, etc.
- Do not try to drink away feelings, thoughts, or visions … they will diminish in time

- Talk to peer support, EAP, clergy, spouse, friends, family, etc.
- Remain active and try to maintain regular schedule and activities

9.4 Reactions to Traumatic Events, Tragedies, and Significant Transitions

There may be times when we experience traumatic events, personal tragedies, or significant transitions. Examples of these types of incidents include injuries, illnesses, assaults, robberies, fires, transportation accidents, natural disasters (hurricanes, earthquakes, tornadoes), death of close friend(s) or loved one(s) due to unusual circumstances, and organizational (layoffs, relocations, etc.) as well as personal transitions (divorce, etc.).

In recent years, a great deal of research has developed around the reactions that people have to these experiences. It has been found that surviving such an event *or just witnessing* the event may leave the individual with some very strong reactions. The following are some of the common reactions that may develop as a result of these types of experiences.

Physical	Emotional	Cognitive
Sleep problems	Anxiety	Memory problems
Eating problems	Fear	Confusion
Minor physical symptoms	Guilt	Difficulty with decisions
Startle responses	Feeling irritable	Intrusive thoughts/visions
Sweating/chills	Feeling remote/numb	
Fatigue	Sadness	
	Intrusive thoughts/visions	

These are the usual and common reactions to what may be a very difficult and dramatic event in one's life. Not everyone will experience any or all of these reactions; however, if you do, it is important to remember that, for most people, these reactions will diminish over a few days to a few weeks. If not, please seek out additional services.

The following are some hints and strategies that may help you if you have any of these reactions:

- Try to talk to others about your experience.
- Sometimes it is difficult to talk to family or close friends, as it may be upsetting to them. Therefore, use other resources such as staff, colleagues, clergy, and medical and behavioral health professionals.
- Maintain usual social contacts...staying connected to others is important.
- Remain active and try to keep your regular schedule/activities.
- Limit alcohol and other controlled substances.
- If sleep is disturbed, do not toss and turn in bed. Read, watch television, etc.
- Do not think away thoughts, feelings, flashbacks...they will diminish in time.
- Try to increase your level of physical activity and exercise.
- If appetite is disturbed, try to eat small amounts of healthy food.
- Use any other outlets that are of personal value to you as an individual: religion, art, reading, movies, games, yoga, massage, pets, hobbies.
- Do not be afraid to ask for support from others.

On-Site Wellness and Stress Management Programs

Many companies have a variety of stress management and wellness programs available to employees. During tough financial times, these programs are often the first to be cut in an effort to curtail costs. An article by Bette Ann Stead in *Business Horizons,* entitled "Worksite Health Programs: A Significant Cost-Cutting Approach," cites many studies that indicate a significant cost savings derived from employee fitness and wellness programs. This author (Lewis) would strongly urge readers to visit the Web site to review this article and the cost-saving benefits of these programs.[6] As discussed in a previous chapter, workplace toxicity is a constant and efforts to mitigate it must be maintained. When a crisis or tragedy hits a work organization, it can cause a dramatic increase in the toxicity in the workplace and the stress on its employees. Therefore, these programs are an essential component to maintaining a healthy workforce... in good times and in times of crisis. The workplace culture must maintain the attitude that utilization of the programs and facilities is a value that is promoted.

More anecdotal articles and research studies are reporting the benefits of naps or time-out for workers.[7,8] Summarized succinctly by James Maas, author of *Power Sleep: The Revolutionary Program that Prepares Your Mind for Peak Performance,* "Businesses who ignore the financial and health benefits of napping at work are asleep at the switch."[9] This author (Lewis) would suggest that for several months after a workplace crisis, people might experience sleep disruption, fatigue, and difficulties with concentration. Having scheduled time-outs or rest breaks would certainly be a benefit. The often-expressed concern that people would use them inappropriately or unnecessarily is usually a myth. In fact, one might predict that there would be less sick days and perhaps increased productivity during the adjustment phase after a significant crisis in the workplace.

External Resources and Alternative Health Services

In addition to an EAP and on-site wellness programs, it would be important to know what other resources are available in the local professional community. If one has an EAP, ask them about the referral network within the company's insurance carrier. Are alternative forms of healthcare available, such as chiropractic care, physical therapy, massage, etc.? If not, and people wish to avail themselves of these services on their own, does the EAP know of providers?

Employee Feedback

As described, information must have consistency, redundancy, frequency, continuity, and circularity. Information must flow back and forth from management to employees. Oftentimes, management is left in the position of trying to guess at what information the employees want to know rather than going directly to the employees themselves. This author has seen a number of methods by which companies can get useful information. Surveys and focus groups are two relatively easy and not too time-consuming methods of receiving information. However, these methods require someone who is skilled at facilitating these services, otherwise they can turn into a venting free-for-all. This author has seen focus groups used very effectively after a serious incident in which a building was closed down for an extended period of time. Prior to re-entry, focus groups were formed to determine what concerns the returning employees would have, what services they wanted in place to facilitate the transition, etc. For managers, there was another group that looked specifically at their needs. Other focus groups were held over three to six months to determine what the needs were as time progressed. Surveys can be used in much the same manner and then summarized and fed back to the employees. Both of these methods also let the employees know that their feedback and reactions have some value.

Administrative Visibility

As indicated throughout this book, there is nothing quite as valuable as having "face time" with upper management. This author suggests to upper management that they get out of their offices, walk around, and spend informal time with employees. Having coffee, lunch breaks, and drop-in sessions where employees can talk directly with senior staff is strongly urged.

If for any reason a building has been evacuated or damaged or rehabbed, it is important to be sure to repopulate the building from the top down. This would also apply in situations where there has been some criminal activity, such as a bank robbery or a violent event. That is, be sure to bring the employees back by first having administrative personnel return, then department heads, then supervisors, and then regular employees. As each level comes back on line, they may benefit from some consultation and debriefing services. Each level should acclimate to the situation and then be available to facilitate the reentry of the next group.

Keep Your Head above Water (I Mean "de Nile") Take the Time

There is an interesting saying that this author picked up somewhere along the way during consulting: "The higher up the feeding chain your position, the less you really know about what is going on." Or, put another way, "The closer to the head, the less you see and hear." Often, the higher-ups make it clear as to what messages they want to hear from their reports. As if it is a reflection upon them (and it may be) in response to a question from a boss: "How's it going with your department, Smith?" The answer "Fine, boss" may not be totally accurate, yet the subordinate does not feel that he can tell the truth that would be more akin to: "Well, to tell you the truth, the morale is pretty low since the layoff. People are grumbling about the workload and absenteeism has increased in the past month. People are bickering with each other, and some folks have put in for transfers to another department. Other than that... all is great." Many work organizations respond to workplace crises with a "don't ask, don't tell" approach. Or, there may be an initial response, but then the message goes out... "all should be OK, now."

As clearly pointed out throughout this book, crises take time to resolve. Often it is not until two to three months after an incident that the organization may begin to see the true impact of an event. Response plans should be phased in over an extended period of time, depending on the nature and severity of the incident and the assessed impact on employees. Keep eyes, ears, and hearts open.

The Utilization of Consultants

In recent years, emergency management and organizational continuity has spawned a cottage industry of consultants. The focus is diverse, ranging over a myriad of areas such as building security, information technology, "preventing" workplace violence, legal issues, setting up data recovery centers, and employee issues, to name only a few. There are consultants that specialize in certain types of industries or work settings, be it financial, healthcare, education, or manufacturing. Attendance at any of the national business continuity or disaster management conferences will provide a bevy of vendors plying their services.

It is the opinion of this author that, as this is a relatively new and rapidly developing field, no one person or even a small group can cover all the bases. Therefore, availing one's organization of consultation services is at worst a necessary evil and at its best can be a value-added service that can enhance a plan as well as provide support for the BCP team. Oftentimes, a consultant can suggest or say things that internal employees may not feel comfortable to say to "higher-ups." Or, having experience from working with other organizations, the consultant may save valuable time for the BCP team by them not having to "reinvent the wheel." Further, a consultant *should* be aware of the latest technology as well as compliance issues.

Another valuable aspect of working with a consultant is that (hopefully) the consultant might provide a sense of reassurance when there is an incident. It is strongly recommended by this author that most consultation relationships should have a "retainer" component. Even if there is a specific project or goal to the consultation, there should be availability by the consultant to provide ongoing services should a real incident occur. There have been numerous times after this author has provided consultation or training that an organization will call just to "walk through" their response to the situation. Usually, they have provided a comprehensive response to the incident; however, the feedback received is that "it is nice knowing that there is someone outside the system that can provide an objective paradigm." Do not forget that the people on the crisis response team are also vulnerable to the same reactions as any of the other employees. In fact, they may even be more reactive, as it is their plan and their responsibility that is center stage. Therefore, they may have their own reactions to the event as well as having to provide crisis management services and also be subject to judgment regarding the organization's response. This provides a triple layer of stress. Hence, an outside consultant can act as a "debriefer" to the team to facilitate *their* recovery. Never forget that crisis planners are people too.

Vignette 9.5 is a brief commentary on the utilization of consultants written by an individual who has served in the role of a BCP planner as well as a consultant to others.

9.5 Utilization of Consultants

By Angela Devlen

Engaging consultants is particularly valuable if it is for the purpose of leveraging expertise in a specific area rather than for fulfilling resource gaps. In the areas of emergency management, homeland security, crisis management, business continuity, and disaster medicine, it is important to select the appropriate consultant(s) that have experience extending beyond those who have emerged in the post 9/11 era. Depending on the industry and the specific needs of the organization, more than one consultant may be needed for reasons that include the scope of work, type of industry (e.g., healthcare, financial services, and the public sector all have unique challenges) and the type of engagement. Experts in the field may fill specific niches such as natural hazard mitigation, weapons of mass destruction, mass casualty incident planning, planning for disaster drills, psychological elements of disasters, or business continuity for a specific industry. In addition, every organization should design the contract with consultants to provide a sustainable program and offer knowledge transfer that allows them to manage future incidents. Another important consideration is to retain the consultant to provide services during times of emergency. When considering which consultant(s) will best suit your needs, credentials such as those offered by the Disaster Recovery Institute International (CBCP or MBCP) or the International Association of Emergency Managers (CEM) are important. Knowledge of industry standards and regulations is critical. (NFPA 1600, DRII, Incident Command System, OSHA, SEC, Sarbanes-Oxley, etc.). They must have a clear understanding of operational, financial, human, and technological elements and how they are all part of comprehensive emergency management planning. Access to resources and additional experts in specific areas that serve the needs of the organization are also critical. Choosing consultants may be a difficult process; however, those that (1) have spoken at national and international conferences, (2) have been published and interviewed in industry magazines, (3) contribute to or are authors of white papers, (4) serve on the board of industry-specific agencies and organizations, and (5) are supporting the advancement of the field through research and academic program development should be considered leaders in this developing field.

Pioneers in the industry are developing areas that have long since been overlooked, particularly human/psychological factors and private–public sector collaboration. Few consultants have the background or education to deploy programs that include these essential elements of any emergency management program. Without these elements, no plan is complete. No organization is a silo unto itself and during an emergency is dependent on other companies and agencies. Without people, no organization can respond to and recover from an emergency situation. When selecting a consultant, consideration of all of these factors is important to ensure that an organization is truly getting the expertise required to implement such a critical and complex effort. To begin the search to retain a qualified consultant, contact professional organizations or consortia such as DRIE, NEDRIX, and All-Hands for recommendations. Other sources include industry magazines such as *DRJ* and *Continuity Insights,* as these magazines publish articles written by experts in the field. If considering engaging a large firm rather than an independent consultant, request resumes of the members of the team who will be supporting your project and critique them against the criteria laid out above. The success of such a program is not only critical to your organization, but to the safety and welfare of your employees — your most important resource.

The following Web sites may be of assistance:

- Disaster Recovery Institute International: http://www.drii.org/
- International Association of Emergency Managers: http://www.iaem.com/
- Disaster Recovery Information Exchange–Canada: http://www.drie.org/index.asp
- New England Disaster Recovery Information X-Change: http://www.nedrix.com
- *Disaster Recovery Journal:* http://www.drj.com/
- *Continuity Insights:* http://www.continuityinsights.com/
- CPM Group: http://www.contingencyplanning.com/
- All-Hands Consortium: http://allhandsconsulting.com/; http://www.all-hands.net/pn/index.php

Angela Devlen is a business continuity and emergency management consultant. Previously, she led Corporate Disaster Recovery Planning at Partners HealthCare System where she was responsible for leading disaster recovery planning efforts across information systems, establishing a business continuity program, and supporting emergency preparedness efforts for hospitals within Partners. During her 15-year career, she has developed business continuity and emergency management plans for clients in the finance, healthcare, insurance industries and the public sector. She is currently working with Boston University's Metropolitan College and School of Public Health to develop and market programs in business continuity and disaster management. Angela is a speaker at industry conferences and is regularly published and interviewed on the subject of business continuity. Angela is a member of the International Association of Emergency Managers and the New England Disaster Recovery Information Exchange.

In closing, there are probably other services and interventions that could be supplied and utilized to facilitate the recovery of human technology. Each industry and type of work setting must devote time and attention to the specific culture, demographics, and dynamics of their workplace and workforce. While it is impossible to derive a formula for each venue, hopefully this book has generated a thinking process by which to approach the task.

References

1. E. Lindemann, Symptomatology and Management of Acute Grief, American Journal of Psychiatry, 101, 141–148, 1944.
2. A. Kardiner and H. Spiegel, War Stress and Neurotic Illness, Hoeber, New York, 1947.
3. http://www.vnh.org/CombatStress/B5HERDebrief.html.
4. J.T. Mitchell and G.S. Everly, Critical Incident Stress Debriefing, Chevron Publishing, Ellicott City, MD, 1996.
5. G. Lewis, Critical Incident Stress and Trauma in the Workplace, Accelerated Development, 1994.
6. http://www.findarticles.com/p/articles/mi_m1038/is_n6_v37/ai_15911074.
7. N. Turner, Are You Slacking if You're Napping… Maybe Not, http://www.truestarhealth.com/members/cm_archives13ML3P1A10.html.
8. L. Lamberg, When Napping at Work Is Good for You, http://www.psych.org/pnews/00-09-01/napping.html.
9. J. Maas, Power Sleep: The Revolutionary Program that Prepares Your Mind for Peak Performance, Random House and Harper Collins, 1999.

Appendix A

Workbook

As stated, one of the goals of this book is to help readers think through the management and mitigation of potential crises that may befall their workplace. Appendix A presents three scenarios through which the reader can apply "hands-on" knowledge. The first two take place in a hospital setting, the third with a small community bank. While these may not be similar to the reader's work organization, they should still provide the necessary thoughtfulness required to address the human impact of crisis management.

Appendix B allows the reader to assess his or her organization's business continuity plan relative to workforce recovery.

As stated, crisis management should be thought of as a "team sport" that works best when it utilizes input from various people with different roles within an organization. Therefore, these exercises should and can be worked on as a group effort to enhance the business continuity/disaster management planning team.

Scenario 1: The ABC Hospital

ABC Hospital is a community hospital in a suburban area located in a seacoast town in New England. It has about 200 beds. There are six medical-surgical units, a psychiatric unit, a twelve-bed intensive care unit, and an active emergency room. It is a primary care setting; however, serious cases are transported to larger trauma centers located in urban settings.

ABC Hospital is staffed with RNs and LPNs. In addition, there are 30 professional/technical personnel, approximately 25 clerical staff, 15 maintenance workers. Security is outsourced to a private security firm. The medical staff (MDs) consists of 50+ physicians. The administrative staff is made up of a CEO, CFO, COO, MIS Director, Director of HR, Director of Nursing, medical staff officer, Risk Management, and part-time legal consultant.

The make-up of the RN staff is predominantly white female, ranging in age from 20 to 65 years. The LPN staff is more diverse, with about 5 percent African American, 5 percent Latino, and 5 percent Asian descent. Of the RN and LPN staff, approximately 60 percent are regular employees while the remaining are per-diem/contract from a staffing agency. There is a strong nursing and clerical staff union; however, the per-diem staff are not members of it. The major portion of the personnel live within a 25-mile radius and commute by car to the hospital.

Organizational Culture Assessment

Assess the culture, toxicity, dynamics, etc., what other information do you require? Please list other critical questions or information that you may need to determine the organizational culture and its dynamics before proceeding to the next section.

1)

2)

3)

4)

5)

6)

7)

Now that you have listed some of the crucial questions, you can turn to the next page, which will provide you with some pertinent information about the workplace culture of this hospital. Perhaps some of your questions will be answered.

Relevant Information to Help Assess the Organizational Culture of the ABC Hospital

Due to changes with the managed care/insurance reimbursement system, the hospital has had to close a unit (15 beds) a year ago. In addition, they laid off about 10 percent of the nursing and 5 percent of clerical staffs. Since then, through attrition, another 5 percent of nurses have left and have not been replaced. Instead, contract staff have been utilized on an as-needed basis. This has resulted in a "two-class system" between the "regular" staff and the "contract" staff. Most of the regular staff are "townies" who have lived in the area for some time. The contract staff is composed of mainly "out-of-towners" who have little connection to the immediate area. The nursing contract does not apply to the contract staff who work different shift hours and receive more money per hour, but with no benefits or regular schedule.

Benefits have been decreased: (1) cannot carry over vacation; (2) increase in employee contribution to health insurance; (3) no more sponsorship of Christmas party; and (4) units are staffed with less RNs.

Fewer people are using the hospital because they are choosing to go to larger hospitals in a nearby city. The length of hospitalizations has been cut due to insurance limitations, and this has resulted in more acute cases that require greater care, but with less staff available.

The MDs are less available as they are admitting fewer patients due to insurance restrictions and are spending more time in their private offices treating more patients on an out-patient basis. This is not their choice, but rather the mandate from the managed care/insurance carriers. There are no in-house attending physicians (MDs salaried by the hospital to cover patients).

The hospital is actively seeking partnership with or possibly being purchased by several larger institutions. Were this to happen, there is concern that the current staff would lose their seniority to the partnering or purchasing institution.

Nurses as well as clerical staff are in contract negotiations with the hospital, which have not been going well. There is some rumored talk of "working to rule" or "sick-outs" to demonstrate their dissatisfaction with the lack of movement in the contract negotiations. Approximately 20 percent of nursing and clerical staff are "single mothers."

The demographics of the surrounding area have changed significantly in the past 10 to 15 years. Whereas it used to be more of a small-town farming area, it is now becoming more "suburbanized," with new housing developments that cater to upper-middle-class expansion of professional families. More demand has been placed on the hospital to provide higher levels of diagnostic and treatment services, while it is faced with mounting fiscal pressures. As a result, the reputation of the hospital has taken a bit of a hit in the last couple of years and there has been a recent increase in medical malpractice suits against the physicians and the hospital.

Also, there is an ongoing sexual harassment suit between one of the nurses and a physician that has received a fair amount of media coverage.

With this information available, think about the cultural issues as well as the toxic factors in this workplace. Describe several critical aspects of this culture that might impact emergency management and organizational continuity planning.

1)

2)

3)

4)

As part of any organizational continuity plan, one of the first steps is to perform a Risk Assessment or BIA (Business Impact Analysis). What types of disruptions might one expect at a hospital such as this? Please list up to ten types of incidents that you might assume could happen to this hospital.

1)

2)

3)

4)

5)

6)

7)

8)

9)

10)

Chose two or three of the incidents that you believe would have a significant impact on operations of the hospital as well as personnel. Using the questions from Steven Fink's assessment model described in Chapter 3, derive a Crisis Impact Value (CIV) for these incidents. Remember: to derive the CIV, assign a value of 1 to 10 to each one of these questions below:

1. Is the incident likelihood of escalation? _____
2. Is there media, government, regulatory scrutiny? _____
3. Does the incident cause interference with normal operations? _____
4. Is there or could there be a negative impact on public image? _____
5. Could the incident cause damage to organization's bottom line? _____

Total _____

Then divide the total by 5 to derive the CIV. /5

CIV _____

	Event	CIV (1–10)	PF (%)	Quadrant (Hi/Hi, Lo/Lo)
1				
2				
3				

Now, using Fink's Crisis Plotting Grid, plot the likelihood of the three events occurring (see Figure A.1). Once again, remember that this is just

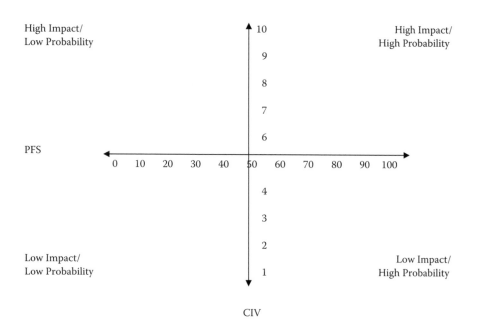

FIGURE A.1 Fink's crisis plotting grid.

a guess, not necessarily an accurate assessment. Plot the incidents on the graph below to determine in which quadrant they would be placed.

Using the Human Factor Assessment tool of the author, first assign the incident to one of the five types of incidents. Then derive a score to determine the potential impact on personnel for the two chosen events. Each factor is assigned a 1 to 10 rating. Remember, scores greater than 50 are considered a high impact.

Incident 1: _____

Incident 1	Man-made I	Man-made II	Natural Disaster	Organizational Transition	Infrastructure Disruption
Locus of impact					
Timing					
Duration					
Impact on operations					
I/D premises					
I/D personnel					
I/D reputation					
I/D residences					
I/D social structure					
Concurrent stressors					
Total score					

Notes:

Locus of impact:

_____

_____

_____

Timing:

_____

_____

_____

Duration:

_____

_____

_____

Impact on operations:

_____

_____

_____

I/D premises:

_____

_____

_____

I/D personnel:

_____

_____

_____

I/D reputation:

_____

_____

_____

I/D residences:

_____

_____

_____

I/D social structure:

_____

_____

_____

Concurrent stressors:

_____

_____

_____

Do the same for Incident 2.

Incident 2: _____

Incident 1	Man-made I	Man-made II	Natural Disaster	Organizational Transition	Infrastructure Disruption
Locus of impact					
Timing					
Duration					
Impact on operations					
I/D premises					
I/D personnel					
I/D reputation					
I/D residences					
I/D social structure					
Concurrent stressors					
Total score					

Notes:

Locus of impact:

_____
_____
_____

Timing:

_____
_____
_____

Duration:

_____
_____
_____

Impact on operations:

_____

_____

_____

I/D premises:

_____

_____

_____

I/D personnel:

_____

_____

_____

I/D reputation:

_____

_____

_____

I/D residences:

_____

_____

_____

I/D social structure:

_____

_____

_____

Concurrent stressors:

_____

_____

_____

Do the same for Incident 3.

Incident 3: _____

Incident 1	Man-made I	Man-made II	Natural Disaster	Organizational Transition	Infrastructure Disruption
Locus of impact					
Timing					
Duration					
Impact on operations					
I/D premises					
I/D personnel					
I/D reputation					
I/D residences					
I/D social structure					
Concurrent stressors					
Total score					

Notes:

Locus of impact:

_____

_____

_____

Timing:

_____

_____

_____

Duration:

_____

_____

_____

Impact on operations:

_____

_____

_____

I/D premises:

_____

_____

_____

I/D personnel:

_____

_____

_____

I/D reputation:

_____

_____

_____

I/D residences:

_____

_____

_____

I/D social structure:

_____

_____

_____

Concurrent stressors:

_____

_____

_____

Human Factor Impact

Now that you have conducted an assessment on these three incidents and you have estimated the areas of impact on personnel, think about how these events could affect the staff (and patients, for that matter). Once again, assess the immediate as well as the long-term potential impact on staff. Perhaps by utilizing the stages/phases paradigm as described in Chapter 5, map out some of the potential repercussions and reactions that can be expected from staff.

Incident 1: _____

Survival phase (0–48 hours):

Support phase (days 2–10):

Adjustment (weeks 2–16):

Resolution (months 6–18):

Re(dis)covery (2 years+):

Incident 2: _____

Survival phase (0–48 hours):

Support phase (days 2–10):

Adjustment (weeks 2–16):

Resolution (months 6–18):

Re(dis)covery (2 years+):

Incident 3: _____

Survival phase (0–48 hours):

Support phase (days 2–10):

Adjustment (weeks 2–16):

Resolution (months 6–18):

Re(dis)covery (2 years+):

Now that you have assessed the potential impact over some time frame, determine what types of services and interventions should and could be in place to mitigate the impact on personnel. Consider pre-incident, short-term, and long-term strategies.

Incident 1:

Pre-incident preparedness:

Post-incident:
  Short term:

  Long term:

Incident 2:

Pre-incident preparedness:

Post-incident:
    Short term:

    Long term:

Incident 3:

Pre-incident preparedness:

Post-incident:
    Short term:

    Long term:

Scenario 2: The ABC Hospital, Different Scenario

It is mid-December and there is a "nor' easter" predicted to hit the coast within 12 hours and is being touted as the "storm of the century." The coastal areas are being evacuated (voluntary) and emergency management, National Guard, and the Red Cross have activated their command centers in response to a potential natural disaster. Strong winds, high tides, and snow are predicted to produce a storm surge that will flood many communities. Schools have closed and announcements have been made for people to stay off the roads as much as possible.

The hospital is preparing for a busy time in the Emergency Room. They have activated the hospital crisis plan, whereby "essential" personnel must remain at or report to work, and "nonessential" personnel are released. The medical staff (MDs) are either coming in to briefly assess their patients or are calling in orders to the nursing staff. Primarily "regular" nursing staff are working as it is part of their contract. Per-diem/contract staff are not considered on the "essential" list or under contract and therefore do not need to report to work.

With the contract negotiations still bogged down, there is resentment among regular staff. Some of the single-parent staff are complaining about not having care for their young children at home. Other staff have elderly parents about whom they are worried. Many are worried about their own personal residences, automobiles, and property as they recall the blizzard of 1978.

Think through how this type of an event might impact the hospital. Once again, look at a business impact analysis (BIA) that encompasses the operational as well as the human impact on this organization.

What are the top three immediate *operational* issues or concerns that must be addressed to keep the hospital functioning?

1)

2)

3)

What are the top three *staff/workforce* concerns or issues?

1)

2)

3)

Once again, speculate as to what would be some immediate strategies to lessen the staff issues/concerns generated from this incident.

Pre-incident preparedness:

Post-incident — short term:

Post-incident — long term:

Scenario 3: The ABC Bank

The ABC Bank is a community banking system with 15 branches located within a three-state region. The bank employs approximately 425 full- and part-time people, most of whom are young female tellers and branch managers. In addition, there are about 55 administrative personnel, ranging from department heads in a wide variety of services such as loans/mortgages, business development, human resource, maintenance, security, information technology, etc., as well as their clerical staff.

Many of the employees grew up and reside in the area, know the customers, and remain working at the bank for many years. For a sizeable portion, it was their first job and they have remained there and worked their way up into administrative positions. The workforce is rather homogeneous, dominated by Caucasian and Catholic demographics. The female tellers and branch managers often get married, take a short-term pregnancy leave, and then return to work, often in part-time positions. The men either move up through the ranks or leave to take higher positions with other banks. While there is a gender bias, this is understood and accepted. The women feel that the bank will work with them to bring them back in some capacity. Also, there is an unwritten/unspoken leniency with respect to the women being able to take time off for sick children, doctor's appointments, etc.

The bank has been in business for more than 75 years and initially was a community bank located in the center of the town catering to the local population. For the past 25 years, the local area has changed with new upper-middle-class housing developments, a large mall, and other commercial development. The bank has made a significant effort to expand geographically as well as in terms of offered services. These efforts were initially generated as some of the "big banks" began to set up branches in the area and created a competitive market for the first time. While this expansion was taking place, the bank has been able to maintain its user-friendly attitude with its customers.

Business has been good and the expansion has gone quite well. There have been no layoffs or any significant fiscal struggles. In fact, the bank has grown from under 200 employees to its current level in the past 15 years. Even with this change, there is a significant social culture among the employees, and many see each other outside the workplace. Further, the bank sponsors a variety of local events, such as a charity golf tournament, a Christmas party, a charity food and toy drive, and sponsorship of Little League teams. The president of the bank, a local man, is also the president of the local Chamber of Commerce as well as a member of the school board and other business boards of directors.

During the past five years, the bank added an EAP as a benefit for employees and their families. During this same time frame, three branches had experienced note-pass robberies with no injuries or significant disruptions. In addition, the bank has added an online capacity that required a huge amount of time and resources, causing much stress, but finally is in place with limited problems. This accomplishment was experienced by all as a significant event as it signaled that the little bank is now "playing with the big banks."

Up until about ten years ago, the IT and security departments were rather small, with limited roles and duties. Since then, these two departments have expanded their roles as well as the number of employees and have developed into two of the major players within the institution. As a result, these two departments head up the disaster management/business continuity planning. Also, they are seen as the departments that have the ear of the Senior Administration, and receive monies whenever needed as they can justify it for security issues. There is a growing disparity between what these departments (especially IT) pay starting employees as compared to other departments.

Once again, think about the culture of this workplace. Clearly, it is an organization in transition. Originally shaped with a small-town, "mom-and-pop" orientation serving the local community, it has recently been undergoing a transmutation as a result of changes in the banking industry, the local and national economies, and concerns regarding security.

Brief Business Impact Analysis

List the three top events that could significantly impact the work organization. Rate the Crisis Impact Value (CIV) as well as a guess as to the Probability Factor of these events. If you prefer, you can use another assessment methodology. (Please note that this is not a complete BIA, but will serve for the purposes of this exercise.)

	Event	CIV (1–10)	PF (%)	Quadrant (Hi/Hi, Lo/Lo)
1				
2				
3				

On Friday morning, the bank president meets with Senior Administrative staff and department heads and announces that the bank will be purchased by another bank. This purchase will take effect in three months' time. While many of the tellers and branch managers, custodial and maintenance staff will be maintained, the middle and upper management positions, security, as well as much of the clerical staff will experience the greatest losses as many of the duties of these positions will be transferred to the new bank administration. Actual numbers and positions will not be known for about four to six weeks.

It is also known that this banking chain has been purchasing a large number of smaller, successful banks over the past ten years. They have expanded rapidly, quadrupling the number of branches, personnel, and services. The orientation of the acquiring bank is quite different than that of ABC Bank. There is no "warm and fuzzy feel" to the organization; in fact, it has a reputation of being more cutthroat, competitive, and callous toward employees. The turnover rate is rather high, especially for employees of former acquisitions. The demand is much higher to provide services, and generate loans and other business.

How would you recommend that the bank handle informing the employees about the upcoming acquisition?

How do you imagine that the workforce will respond to this information?

The president has indicated that he will be retiring as a result of this transition. Many of the Senior Administrative staff as well as department heads will not have positions in the new bank. Yet, this information is vague and the specifics are not known. However, the president has requested that the group meet to develop a "transition plan" (he does not like to call it a crisis plan as it sounds too dramatic).

Describe below some of the short- and long-term interventions and strategies that the team should suggest.

Appendix B

Assessment of Organization and Organizational Continuity Plan

Having taken the time to go through the simulation exercises in Appendix A, now take an assessment of your own work organization and its Organizational Continuity Plan.

1. Assess Your Organization's Continuity Planning Committee

What is your committee called?

Who are the members of your Business Continuity Planning Committee, Crisis Planning Committee, Disaster Response Committee?

__ IT
__ HR
__ Security
__ Risk management
__ COO

__ Legal
__ EAP
__ Labor
__ Public relations
__ Outside consultant
__ Other: _____

Who is the "head" of the team/committee? _____

How was this person chosen for this role? Experience and knowledge?
Seniority? Title/position?
_____
_____
_____

How often does this committee/team meet?

__ 1 × per year __ 2 × per year __ 4 × per year __ More often

How much money is budgeted annually for your BCP, DM, CM planning
activities? _____

How is this money utilized? Training for committee members? Simulations?
Other uses?

Where is your plan "kept"?

How has the plan been communicated to supervisors and employees?

Is your plan "tested" or "walked through"? Are there drills?
How often?

Briefly describe the auditing procedure(s) for your plan.

Does the audit in any way look at the impact on personnel, or is it primarily oriented toward operations and IT?

Notes:

2. Assess Your Workplace Culture

How long has your company been in business (in its current form)? _____

What type of environment?

__ Factory
__ Manufacturing
__ Office setting
__ Healthcare institution
__ Educational institution
__ Governmental/municipal
__ Financial/insurance
__ IT/software development
__ Sales
__ Other: _____

Geographic factors:

__ Local
__ Regional
__ National
__ International

Briefly describe:

_____
_____
_____

Bargaining units/labor unions/associations: _____ Yes _____ No

Publicly held (stock): _____ Yes _____ No

Number of employees:
_____ Full-time   ____ Male   ____ Female
_____ Part-time   ____ Male   ____ Female

Ethnicity/race: (feel free to estimate)

African/American   ____ % Male   ____ % Female
Latino   ____ % Male   ____ % Female
Caucasian   ____ % Male   ____ % Female
Asian   ____ % Male   ____ % Female
Other   ____ % Male   ____ % Female

Education level:
___ % High school
___ % College
___ % Graduate training

Age groups:
___ % 20-something
___ % 30-something
___ % 40-something
___ % 50-something
___ % 60-something

Average length of employment with this organization:

___ % 0 to 3 years ___ % 3 to 5 years ___ % 6 to 8 years ___ % 8+ years

During the past three years, please check off which of these toxicity-producing incidents or events have occurred in the workplace:

__ Layoff(s)
__ Merger
__ Acquisition of another company
__ Acquired by another company
__ Decrease in benefits
__ Mandatory overtime
__ Relocation of significant portion of workforce (more than 15 miles)
__ Personnel change in upper management
__ Significant change in demographics of a portion of the workforce (e.g., ethnic, gender, age, etc.)
__ Work that was once done by "inside" employees has been outsourced
__ Lawsuits against the organization or any of its employees

__ Violent incidents
__ Other criminal or civil activities (sexual harassment, sabotage, embez-
zlement, etc.)
__ Strikes/work action, etc.
__ Damage to reputation
__ Significant number of terminations of employees for cause
__ If labor unions are involved, has there been an increase in grievances?

Now take a look at any positive factors that might improve morale. Does
your workplace offer any of the following:

__ EAP/wellness programs
__ Time-out rooms
__ Daycare
__ Health club
__ Sports teams
__ Informal social activities
__ Organization-sponsored social events
__ Bonuses
__ Merit increases
__ Cost-of-living increases
__ Organization-sponsored charity events
__ Other: _____
_____

Take a moment to describe the social milieu of your organization by
answering these questions:

Is it "cliquey"?

Do people eat together in a cafeteria or in isolation at their workstations?

Does management have an "open-door" attitude, or is it by appointment
only?

Do people feel comfortable going to Human Resources?

Do groups of people socialize outside of work?

Is there rapid turnover of staff?

Are people promoted from within and therefore rise up through the
ranks of the organization, or must they leave to gain further professional
status?

Is there interdepartmental communication and cooperation? Or, is it more of a "siloed" or "smoke stacked" workplace where each department tends to work alone?

Is there any type of holiday season festivities sponsored by the workplace? Is it well attended?

Does your workplace have a favorite charity or fund that it likes to support?

Are there any other events or demonstrations of the sort that benefits the morale of the workers?

Now, with this data available, spend some time to briefly (and objectively) describe the social and cultural milieu of your workplace. Consider whether it is a highly stressful environment with much toxicity; or, although it may be very busy and hard working with long hours, is there is a cooperative attitude among the workers? Describe the co-worker–to–co-worker relationships. How about interdepartmental communication? Is management respected by non-management (and vice versa)?

3. Assessment of Pre-impact Preparedness

Does your workplace have any of the following policies?
__ Sexual harassment
__ Workplace violence with restraining order
__ Drug and alcohol
__ Evacuation
__ Shelter in place
__ IT Security
__ Other: _____

How are these policies displayed, distributed, posted, and made available to employees?

Does your workplace provide training for supervisors and education of employees around the aforementioned policies and protocols?

If so, how often?

If not, why not?

Does your organization have practice evacuation and shelter-at-work drills?

If so, how often?

If not, why not?

If your workplace has "essential" personnel that must be immediately available at times of crisis or emergency, are there policies, protocols, or plans in place to help them with their personal and familial needs? If so, please describe:

What type of communication system is in place to provide employees with immediate information regarding an acute organizational continuity incident?

1)

2)

3)

4)

5)

What type(s) of communication system is available to provide employees with ongoing information regarding the resolution of an organizational continuity incident?

1)

2)

3)

4)

5)

Does your organization utilize the services of outside consultants? If so, please describe the nature of their consultation. Are they available to provide services at times of real disruption?

4. Brief Business Impact Analysis

List the five top events that could significantly impact your work organization. Rate the Crisis Impact Value (CIV) as well as a guess as to the Probability Factor of these events. If you prefer, you can use another assessment methodology. (Please note that this is not a complete BIA, but will serve for the purposes of this exercise.)

	Event	*CIV* *(1–10)*	*PF* *(%)*	*Quadrant* *(Hi/Hi, Lo/Lo)*
1				
2				
3				
4				
5				

5. Human Factor Assessment

Using the Human Factor Assessment tool developed by this author, appraise the potential impact on the workforce by rating each of these factors with a 1 to 10 rating. Remember that a score greater than 50 is considered significant.

Incident 1	Man-made I	Man-made II	Natural Disaster	Organizational Transition	Infrastructure Disruption
Locus of impact					
Timing					
Duration					
Impact on operations					
I/D premises					
I/D personnel					
I/D reputation					
I/D residences					
I/D social structure					
Concurrent stressors					
Total score					

Notes:

Incident 2	Man-made I	Man-made II	Natural Disaster	Organizational Transition	Infrastructure Disruption
Locus of impact					
Timing					
Duration					
Impact on operations					
I/D premises					
I/D personnel					
I/D reputation					
I/D residences					
I/D social structure					
Concurrent stressors					
Total score					

Notes:

Incident 3	Man-made *I*	Man-made *II*	*Natural Disaster*	*Organizational Transition*	*Infrastructure Disruption*
Locus of impact					
Timing					
Duration					
Impact on operations					
I/D premises					
I/D personnel					
I/D reputation					
I/D residences					
I/D social structure					
Concurrent stressors					
Total score					

Notes:

Incident 4	Man-made *I*	Man-made *II*	*Natural Disaster*	*Organizational Transition*	*Infrastructure Disruption*
Locus of impact					
Timing					
Duration					
Impact on operations					
I/D premises					
I/D personnel					
I/D reputation					
I/D residences					
I/D social structure					
Concurrent stressors					
Total score					

Notes:

Incident 5	Man-made I	Man-made II	Natural Disaster	Organizational Transition	Infrastructure Disruption
Locus of impact					
Timing					
Duration					
Impact on operations					
I/D premises					
I/D personnel					
I/D reputation					
I/D residences					
I/D social structure					
Concurrent stressors					
Total score					

Notes:

6. Interventions

Now, if any of these have been assessed with scores higher than 50, please set up strategies and responses to mitigate the impact on the workforce and their families.

Once again, consider pre-impact preparedness, and post-impact short- and long-term approaches.

Pre-impact preparedness:

Post-impact — short term:

Post-impact — long term:

Summary:

Please describe future goals or areas of development for your organization's crisis management plan.

1)

2)

3)

4)

5)

6)

7)

8)

Index